Math, Culture, and Popular Media

Activities to Engage Middle School Students Through Film, Literature, and the Internet

Michaele F. Chappell

Denisse R. Thompson

HEINEMANN • PORTSMOUTH, NH

Heinemann
361 Hanover Street
Portsmouth, NH 03801–3912
www.heinemann.com

Offices and agents throughout the world

The authors and publisher wish to thank those who have generously given permission to reprint borrowed material:

Excerpts from "A Raisin in the Sun: Fostering Cultural Connections with a Classic Movie" by Michaele F. Chappell and Denisse R. Thompson. Originally printed in *Mathematics Teaching in the Middle School*, December 2000, Volume 6, Issue 4. Reprinted by permission of the National Council of Teachers of Mathematics.

Excerpts from "Exploring Mathematics Through Asian Folktales" by Denisse R. Thompson, Michaele F. Chappell, and Richard A. Austin from *Changing the Faces of Mathematics: Perspectives on Asian American and Pacific Islanders* edited by Walter G. Secada and Carol A. Lewis. Copyright © 1999 by the National Council of Teachers of Mathematics. Published by the National Council of Teachers of Mathematics. Reprinted by permission of the publisher.

Library of Congress Cataloging-in-Publication Data
Chappell, Michaele F.
  Math, culture, and popular media : activities to engage middle school students through film, literature, and the Internet / Michaele F. Chappell, Denisse R. Thompson.
    p. cm.
  Includes bibliographical references.
  ISBN-13: 978-0-325-02122-5
  ISBN-10: 0-325-02122-8
  1. Mathematics—Study and teaching (Middle school)—Activity programs.
I. Thompson, Denisse R.   II. Title.
  QA11.2.C435 2009
  510.71'2—dc22

2009006135

Editor: Emily Michie Birch
Production: Elizabeth Valway
Technology developer: Nicole Russell
Cover design: Lisa Fowler
Composition: Publishers' Design and Production Services, Inc.
Manufacturing: Valerie Cooper

Printed in the United States of America on acid-free paper
13 12 11 10 09   VP   1 2 3 4 5

Dedicated to my siblings, *Olivayon* and *Preston,* for their love and encouragement.
In loving memory of my *mother* and *father,* for having always inspired me to learn.

—*Michaele*

Dedicated to my parents for always believing in me and providing their love and support.

—*Denisse*

Contents

Investigations by Content
and Culture

Resource F=Film B=Books	Number & Operations	Algebraic Thinking	Geometry	Measurement	Data Analysis & Probability
African and African American					
Akeelah and the Bee (F)	• Learning New Words	• Learning New Words			• The Luck of the Draw • More About Spelling Bees
No More Baths (F)	• Share Buying • Playground Design	• Share Buying	• Playground Design	• Playground Design	
The Pursuit of Happyness (F)	• Getting Rid of the Machines • Making Cold Calls	• Getting Rid of the Machines			• Numbers in Your Head • Solving the Rubik's Cube
A Raisin in the Sun (F)		• All in a Day's Work			• Housing Prices and Costs • Math Survey
Beatrice's Goat (B)	• Goat Figure • Adopt a Goat			• Goat Figure	
The Black Snowman (B)	• Making Money Through Recycling			• Snowman: Here Today, Gone Tomorrow • Making Money Through Recycling	• Snowman: Here Today, Gone Tomorrow • Avoiding Accidents
A Million Fish . . . More or Less (B)	• Fish Loss	• Fish Loss		• Turkey Statistics • Stocking an Aquarium	• Turkey Statistics
Senefer (B)	• Multiplication by Senefer			• Obelisks Outstanding	• Obelisks Outstanding
Village of Round and Square Houses (B)			• House Shape	• House Shape • Cover and Recover	
Vision of Beauty (B)	• Company Earnings • Products and Profits • It's All About "Style"				
Why Mosquitoes Buzz in People's Ears (B)		• Actions and Consequences • Logic Rules			• The Buzz on Mosquitoes
Native American and Indigenous Peoples					
The Lost Child (F)	• Weaving on the Loom • Dyeing Wool	• Weaving on the Loom	• Rug Design	• Weaving on the Loom	
Rabbit-Proof Fence (F)	• A Really Long Fence	• Walking a Long Distance	• A Really Long Fence	• A Really Long Fence • Walking a Long Distance	
Spirit of the Animals (F)	• Whales and More Whales • An Eagle Success Story			• Whales and More Whales • Eagle Essentials	• Whales and More Whales • An Eagle Success Story
Seeing the Circle (B)			• Constructing Circles • Will the Hidden Polygons Please Show Up?	• Sizing Up Circles	
The Cherokee (B)	• Corn Craze	• Plentiful Harvest		• Winding Trails	
Arrow to the Sun (B)	• Aiming to Go Far		• Is It Art? Is It Math? • Arrow Attributes • Growing in Stature	• Growing in Stature	

Resource F=Film B=Books	Number & Operations	Algebraic Thinking	Geometry	Measurement	Data Analysis & Probability
Buffalo Woman (B)			• Reflections in the River • Tipi Sizes	• Tipi Sizes	
Latino					
Selena (F)	• Are You in My Space? • Start Up That Band!	• Start Up That Band! • Fashionable Fashions	• Fashionable Fashions	• Are You in My Space?	• Are You in My Space?
Under the Same Moon (F)	• Tomatoes, Tomatoes, Tomatoes • Taking a Trip	• Do You Have Enough Money?		• Tomatoes, Tomatoes, Tomatoes	
First Day in Grapes (B)	• Mind-Full-Paper-Less Counting • Crates of Grapes	• Crates of Grapes			
Harvesting Hope (B)	• Walk for the Cause • Factor in the Farmers				• Factor in the Farmers
Abuela's Weave (B)	• Fair Trade at the Marketplace		• Patterns in the Weave		
Piñatas & Smiling Skeletons (B)	• Mexican Sweets			• Piñatas and Aguinaldos • Mexican Sweets	
Asian and Pacific Islanders					
Children of Heaven (F)	• Lavash Bread			• Lavash Bread • Winning a Place in the Race	• Shoes, Shoes, and More Shoes
The Way Home (F)	• A Day at the Market	• A Day at the Market	• Giving Directions	• Backpacking with Shoulder Poles	• Hang Dry
Issunbōshi (B)	• Living Life One Inch Tall • Timing a Journey			• Living Life One Inch Tall • Timing a Journey	
Munna and the Grain of Rice (B)	• How a Little Becomes a Lot • Weighty Rice	• How a Little Becomes a Lot		• Weighty Rice	
The Adventures of Marco Polo (B)	• Great Are the Numbers	• Postal Relay	• Postal Relay	• Great Are the Numbers	
A Grain of Rice (B)	• The Peasant Problem Solver • Preparing a Feast	• The Peasant Problem Solver		• Storing a Fortune	• Preparing a Feast
Internet Resources (All Cultures)					
Masks of the World			• Same difference • Sym . . . Sym . . . Symmetry	• Cover Your Mask	
Flags of the World	• Watch Out for "Red Flags" • Flags of "Golden" Proportions		• Flag Facts • Colorful Percentages	• Colorful Percentages	• Watch Out for "Red Flags"
Games from Around the World	• Get Your Game On		• Hopping on a Scotch • Making a Soccer Ball		• Hopping on a Scotch • Soccer Gone Global

Preface

We are very excited that you are reading this book! For the past five years, we have purposely viewed films, read children's books, toured museums, and searched websites in preparation for developing this teacher resource. Although there are several meanings that one could extract from the title, *Math, Culture, and Popular Media: Activities to Engage Middle School Students Through Film, Literature, and the Internet,* our primary purpose for writing this resource is straightforward: to make available a user-friendly collection of investigations for middle-grades teachers who want to take advantage of the cultural dynamics that exist in their classrooms. Given the expansion of racially, ethnically, and culturally diverse pre K–12 classrooms, it has become increasingly crucial to acknowledge the interrelationship between culture and mathematics. All students need opportunities to value mathematics and recognize its importance to the larger society using their own cultural lens and perspective. Yet, we know that many teachers have limited time to locate appropriate culturally based media resources and use them to develop suitable mathematics investigations. This book helps solve the time issue by providing numerous investigations that accentuate the connections between mathematics and culture through the use of popular media.

Whenever we have mentioned this project to others, whether educators or not, we are often asked how we developed the idea to link mathematics and culture through media. Our interest started in the mid-1990s when we, along with many other educators, began using children's literature in the elementary mathematics classroom and with our elementary preservice teachers. With the surge of interest in children's literature to teach mathematics, authors began writing books addressing advanced mathematics topics. As a result, we considered how to use such resources with middle-grades students. Our initial forays into middle-grades classrooms with children's literature or other media were successful. When we realized that few resources demonstrating how to make these literature connections within the middle-grades mathematics classroom existed, the idea for this resource was born. With growing concerns to create culturally relevant classrooms to heighten all students' interests and achievement in mathematics, we decided to broaden our focus to address culture as well as mathematics.

We began our collaborative efforts exploring print literature with an African American perspective that provided opportunities for students to engage with mathematics using such resources. As we learned that students were interested and motivated by stories, we expanded our resources to include other media, including entertaining films, museum-quality posters, and culturally based games. Using these powerful tools in classrooms broadens students' interests toward mathematics. In recent years, due to the access of resources via the World Wide Web, we have incorporated the Internet into our work as well. More importantly, we broadened our collection of resources to focus on media representing other dominant cultures of students often attending middle schools. That is, in addition to resources featuring African and African American cultures, we include resources featuring the cultures of Native Americans and Indigenous Peoples, Asian Americans and Pacific Islanders, and Latinos.

We have often had the privilege to work with middle-grades teachers to implement specific investigations in their mathematics classrooms. We have found that using media with a cultural focus enables multiple content strands to be addressed within a single lesson. So, exploring these resources is a viable way for students to study many content topics in a limited amount of time while addressing the learning outcomes in their state standards in an integrated manner. In the process, students appreciate seeing people who resemble them in some way and can identify with primary characters in the stories and scenes.

Math, Culture, and Popular Media is not intended to represent a full mathematics curriculum or to replace a classroom mathematics curriculum. This is an important point to consider when using this resource. Rather, *Math, Culture, and Popular Media* is meant to augment the existing mathematics curriculum by bringing cultural relevancy to the middle-grades mathematics classroom. Certainly this resource can be used in many different ways and in varied school programs (e.g., public, private, parochial, home, charter, single-gender schools). The resource helps bring the perspectives of other cultures into the classroom and provides teachers with investigations that easily mesh with any existing curriculum program.

So regardless of whether you are just beginning the journey of weaving mathematics and culture in your classroom or have been integrating a cultural component into your classroom for some time, we trust you will find the media resources and the mathematics investigations in this book valuable to you and to your students for many years to come. We invite you to share your experiences with us.

Michaele F. Chappell
Middle Tennessee State University
Murfreesboro, TN

Denisse R. Thompson
University of South Florida
Tampa, FL

Acknowledgments

From Michaele and Denisse

The two of us have long had an interest in the use of media to acknowledge the role of culture in the mathematics classroom. Conversations with teachers at numerous mathematics conferences who were interested in integrating culture and mathematics, but who lacked resources, convinced us to begin development of this resource. Our early endeavors to weave mathematics and culture through media in middle-grades classrooms led us to believe that such integration was truly possible. To those teachers who welcomed us into their classrooms or who attended our sessions at conferences and encouraged us to develop this resource, we say "Many thanks."

An unusual resource like this one does not come to fruition without an editor who has the foresight to believe in the potential of the project and who encourages its publication. We especially thank Emily Birch at Heinemann for all her support in turning the dream of this project into reality. We also appreciate the efforts of Elizabeth Valway for her guidance throughout the production process.

From Michaele

For their consistent encouragement to complete this book and their labor through prayer, I wish to thank members of H.O.P.E (especially Alice, Olivayon, and Sandy) and other family and friends (Willie, Mary, Connie, Faye, Catherine, and the Destiny Center). Furthermore, I am grateful for the support extended by Middle Tennessee State University in granting me a semester sabbatical to complete this project. I extend much appreciation to Denisse, a genuine friend and colleague for many years, for envisioning this book with me and for the plentiful discussions (as well as enjoyment) we had while developing it.

From Denisse

My colleagues know I always have numerous projects in various stages of completion; work on different projects ebbs and flows depending on deadlines. So, I especially want to thank Char and Rick for their patience and forbearance as the timeline for my project with them lengthened so that this resource could be finished. My friendship with Michaele has grown over the years as we have collaborated on many endeavors; our frequent discussions about culture have enriched my perspectives on this important issue. I particularly appreciate her support through all the writing to bring this resource to completion.

Introduction

As you think about the title of this resource, *Math, Culture, and Popular Media,* you may wonder *why* a teacher should weave mathematics and culture through media resources and *how* a teacher should select culturally based media resources to engage students in mathematics learning. This resource provides answers to both of these questions. In addition to theoretical perspectives to answer the *why* and *how* questions, we provide practical suggestions for the selection and integration of culture and mathematics. Then, we illustrate this integration through specific investigations tied to films, children's books, and Internet resources.

The chapters in *Math, Culture, and Popular Media* are grouped according to their purpose or the type of resource they highlight. The first two chapters address philosophical, theoretical, and practical perspectives of the *why* and *how* questions of culture and mathematics integration. Moreover, both a cultural index and a mathematics index are introduced to guide the selection of media.

The actual investigations, the major focus of the book, are found in Chapter 3 through Chapter 33. Thirty-one different media resources provide the context for over eighty-five different investigations spanning the range of topics taught in the middle-grades mathematics classroom. Each chapter presents a summary of the resource, including a description and our perspective on the cultural and mathematics indexes, the mathematics focus of the different investigations, and a teacher commentary on each investigation. Collectively, the resources highlight four cultural groups: African and African American; Native American and Indigenous Peoples; Latino; and Asian and Pacific Islanders.

As we developed the investigations, we were guided by the content recommendations for grades 6–8 in the *Principles and Standards for School Mathematics* (National Council of Teachers of Mathematics 2000). By using these recommendations as a reference, we ensure that the investigations are appropriate for a range of students across varied school settings.

Chapter 34 through Chapter 36 conclude the book by discussing how these investigations can be used across disciplines and to integrate multiple cultures. It is not uncommon for middle schools to have times throughout the year when there is a focus on an interdisciplinary unit; these final chapters contain suggestions on how media resources and culture can serve as a basis for a unit that crosses disciplines. Six previously published investigations related to the themes of these chapters are discussed.

There are several other features that will benefit users of this resource. On pages xii–xiii is a matrix that cross-references the investigations by the five content strands in the *Principles and Standards* as well as by culture and media type. This matrix is a quick reference for users to identify an investigation or resource with a particular focus.

We are particularly pleased that all the investigations are contained on the accompanying CD-ROM as Word documents. This feature gives teachers easy access to the investigations and makes it possible for teachers to make adjustments as needed to meet the needs of their students. The Table of Contents on the CD-ROM enables teachers to access the investigations from multiple routes—resource title, cultural group, or media type. We believe this tool complements the book and helps make the integration of mathematics and culture through the use of media resources all the more easily accomplished.

We reiterate that *Math, Culture, and Popular Media* is not intended to serve as the sole middle-grades mathematics curriculum. Rather, the book is a collection of investigations designed to supplement an existing curriculum. We encourage you to use the book at different points throughout the year as the investigations connect with the content of your curriculum. As you become more aware of culturally based resources and how to use them in the classroom, we believe you will begin to recognize other culturally based media resources to add to your repertoire of resources for the mathematics classroom.

Reference

National Council of Teachers of Mathematics. 2000. *Principles and Standards for School Mathematics.* Reston, VA: National Council of Teachers of Mathematics.

Weaving Mathematics and Culture

The chapters in this section provide a background for integrating mathematics and culture through media. In particular, Chapter 1 establishes rationale for a culturally relevant curriculum in middle-grades mathematics classrooms. We also build a case for why we believe a teacher should practice using culturally relevant pedagogy. Of course, having a desire to use materials that would promote a culturally relevant classroom environment is of no value if there exist no relevant materials a teacher could use. This book offers a convenient and practical resource for teachers as they promote such an environment.

Chapter 2 outlines two indexes that we created to guide our selection of media resources: an A-B-C cultural index and an E-I mathematics index. In this chapter, we also provide some practical "how-to" options for integrating the investigations into an existing curriculum. We discuss how lengthy film resources as well as shorter print resources can be used and how Internet resources can facilitate the integration of multiple cultures into the classroom.

CHAPTER 1

Why Weave Culture and Mathematics Through Media?

We recognize that your interest in this book may stem from a desire to learn more about cultural perspectives on teaching mathematics or from a desire to obtain resources enabling you to enhance your current teaching practices in this area. Regardless of your interests, you may find it beneficial to understand the framework supporting, and our rationale for developing, this resource. So in this chapter, we briefly share our thoughts on the blending of culture, mathematics, and media, including why we consider this resource a helpful tool to adopt and maintain a cultural perspective while teaching middle-grades mathematics.

Thoughts on Culture

Thinking solely about the term *culture* can prompt varied meanings and interpretations—some rather broad and others fairly limited in scope. Within the education community, the term *culture* is used unreservedly in numerous contexts without necessarily considering the subtexts surrounding the verbal, written, or nonspoken communication about it. Though it is beyond the scope of this book to elaborate on the notion of culture, we use the comprehensive definition of culture provided by Davis (2006, 4): "the totality of ideas, beliefs, values, activities, and knowledge of a group or individuals who share historical, geographical, religious, racial, linguistic, ethnic, or social traditions, and who transmit, reinforce, and modify those traditions." This definition is dynamic and resonates with our discussions about the notion of culture as it relates to this resource we have developed. Realizing that middle-grades students bring to classrooms different experiences that shape their meanings about mathematics, both from inside and outside the classroom, it seems that embracing culture with its complex factors (e.g., family, gender, language, social class, race, or ethnicity) is one important way to address a need in schools—that is, high achievement in mathematics by all students.

While considering what culture *is*, it is just as necessary to consider what culture *is not*. The Diversity in Mathematics Education Center for Learning and Teaching (DME-CLT) (2007) notes that culture does not equal race or vice versa. The same motto applies to culture and any of its factors—that is, one should not reduce culture to family, ethnicity, gender, or social-class issues. According to Campbell (1996), culture is not artifacts, nor traits or facts, nor music, dance, or holiday heritages; nor is it something bought, sold, or distributed. Instead, culture encompasses negotiations between individuals in their daily activities (DMECLT 2007). Wiest (2001) regards culture similarly, commenting that it "lies much more at the heart of a people than it does in foods eaten or style of dress. Culture is much more integrally intertwined with a group of people, pervading the whole of who they are and strongly influencing their worldview, manner of thinking and communicating, and other ways of processing and interacting with the world around them" (16).

Thoughts on Culture and Mathematics Teaching and Learning

The "totality" and "sharing" that Davis (2006) speaks about result in natural links between culture and mathematics teaching and learning. In fact, Presmeg (2007) discusses the pivotal role culture plays in the teaching and learning of mathematics. When the totality of students' ideas, their beliefs and values they bring to the classroom, their day-to-day activities, and their knowledge are understood and shared appropriately, then students' culture can contribute to their academic success (DMECLT 2007). However, particularly in American schools, many students rarely have opportunities in mathematics classrooms to share, let alone reinforce or modify, their cultural traditions in ways that contribute to their success. In today's environment, students should realize the importance of culture—their own culture as well as the culture of others—in shaping their overall learning goals and outcomes in life. As a result, a multicultural perspective helps students draw on their own experiences, recognize different cultural heritages, combat racism, and promote "socially desirable" attitudes (Joseph 1993, 20–22).

Calls for a Multicultural Perspective in Teaching

For more than a decade, educators have called for school mathematics to be relevant to the lives and culture of students in all grades (Ladson-Billings 1995; Smith and Silver 1995; Tate 1995). Culturally relevant teaching, pioneered by Ladson-Billings (1994), validates the culture (along with its related factors) that students bring to the classroom. In particular, Ladson-Billings (1995) contends that the teacher's role is absolutely essential in making the mathematics classroom culturally relevant because students are influenced more by the *way* teachers teach than *what* they teach. In her vast contribution toward a call for a more multicultural approach to teaching mathematics, Zaslavsky (1996) views multicultural education as a way for teachers to empower students to develop the needed skills to solve problems they are likely to encounter in life.

Wiest (2001) identifies and discusses four major approaches that support mathematics teaching from a multicultural perspective. Teachers should ensure that students: (1) see the portrayal of cultural groups in instructional materials; (2) study historical roots and the evolution of mathematical concepts; (3) examine the formal as well as informal mathematical practices of various cultures; and (4) use mathematics as a tool to study social and cultural phenomena (18–21). In order to cultivate a comprehensive multicultural perspective in the classroom, Wiest suggests that teachers should wisely choose additional resources to supplement basic classroom materials. Through varied mathematical investigations, students can examine a broad range of real and relevant sociocultural issues, which helps foster a multicultural classroom atmosphere.

Although adjustments in the curriculum are perhaps the most convenient changes to make toward cultivating a culturally relevant classroom (Davidson and Cramer 1997), cultivating such an environment extends beyond curriculum changes and the implementation of different types of activities. Ladson-Billings (1994) indicates that the teacher must be the driving force that brings about this change. Davidman and Davidman (1994) provide practical ways to teach with a multicultural perspective and assert that it is important for a teacher to see that "a classroom becomes a *multicultural setting* when the students in that room experience a multicultural curriculum" (8). This setting is established by the teacher's own state of mind, ways of seeing the world, learned behaviors, and beliefs about multiculturalism. Teachers need a heart for a multicultural environment before they consider implementation.

Because mathematics classrooms consist of students from varied cultural backgrounds and are more or less multicultural in the sense of ethnic and cultural groups (Davidman and Davidman 1994), it is essential that multicultural content be integrated into the curriculum at all grade levels. Regardless of the ethnic, racial, or social-class demographics of the school or classroom, culturally based classroom materials are important (Wiest 2001). Specifically, the curriculum needs to incorporate contributions to mathematics by people of all cultures and depict how people of different cultures use mathematics in real-world situations. This ensures that students have opportunities to examine the mathematical contributions of many cultures and, in particular, examine the mathematical uses and contributions within their own personal culture (Shirley 1995). "Exposing students to the contributions of members of their own and other cultures can help them gain confidence, self-esteem, and a sense of belonging, as well as respect for the mathematical thinking of all cultures" (Wiest 2001, 22).

Our Perspective on Culture in This Resource

Several resources exist in which authors begin with some cultural or historical aspect of mathematics and build investigations around those aspects (see, for example, Zaslavsky 1996). For instance, authors might start with Babylonian base 60 numerals or Incan drawings and build mathematics investigations around these concepts. We have taken a slightly different perspective. We first identified resources that highlight individuals from one of four cultural groups living their normal everyday lives; most of these resources are based on modern-day contemporary life although a few are from earlier eras or from classical times. We then created mathematics investigations related to problems or situations these individuals might solve while living their lives. So, students have an opportunity to observe the lives of individuals from different cultures and consider problems that might be relevant to people from those cultures. Culture then becomes a subtle way of addressing mathematics from a nontypical perspective.

Thoughts on the Use of Media to Weave Culture and Mathematics

Resources, such as theatrical films, printed literature books, and the Internet, represent popular media tools with which students frequently interact; in fact, students are becoming increasingly dependent on the use of Internet resources (e.g., consider students' use of Facebook, MySpace, and Google searches). These varied media can be used to create or enhance lessons, therefore increasing students' engagement in mathematical tasks and connecting mathematics to their lives and surroundings. Moreover, through use of culturally based media, teachers can help students communicate across cultural groups.

Media often reflect the cultural nature of a group or individuals in daily surroundings. Sometimes those reflections are positive and sometimes they are negative depending on who develops the media. Today's students are very familiar with media, including films, the Internet, and handheld electronic tools (e.g., MP3 players, iPods, cell phones with text-messaging capabilities). What more powerful way to establish a cultural perspective in the classroom than to use these media resources! Although inaccurate stereotypes may be used at times, teachers can select resources that minimize stereotypes and beliefs so that students reflect positively on the ideas, values, beliefs, and behaviors portrayed through the main characters in the selected media.

Benefits for Students of Using Media to Weave Culture and Mathematics

We believe there are many potential benefits for students in exploring mathematics from a cultural perspective introduced through media (film, print, or Internet resources):

- Students see connections to people who resemble them.

- Students see people who resemble them involved in situations that require critical thinking processes such as problem solving, reasoning, or communication.

- Students see that people with similar cultural experiences resolve problems in particular ways.

- Students see that people of similar cultural experiences created and developed mathematics.

- Students become engaged with mathematics because the tasks have meaning to everyday life.

As a consequence of weaving culture and mathematics through media, students become more culturally aware of themselves and others and realize that all peoples need to be mathematically literate.

Concluding Thoughts

As you embark on exploring the culturally based resources and investigations in this book, we offer a word of caution. Highlighting culture in the mathematics classroom is not for the faint of heart. When teachers use investigations that draw upon cultural differences, they need to be prepared for uncomfortable questions to arise as students confront their own biases. However, the opportunity exists for mature discussions and for students to grow in their own knowledge and understanding of other peoples. We are all better for the effort.

References

Campbell, Duane E. 1996. *Choosing Democracy: A Practical Guide to Multicultural Education.* Upper Saddle River, NJ: Prentice Hall.

Davidman, Leonard, and Patricia T. Davidman. 1994. *Teaching with a Multicultural Perspective: A Practical Guide.* New York: Longman.

Davidson, Ellen, and Leslie Cramer. 1997. "Integrating with Integrity: Curriculum, Instruction, and Culture in the Mathematics Classroom." In *Multicultural and Gender Equity in the Mathematics Classroom: The Gift of Diversity,* edited by Janet Trentacosta and Margaret J. Kenney, 131–41. Reston, VA: National Council of Teachers of Mathematics.

Davis, Bonnie M. 2006. *How to Teach Students Who Don't Look Like You: Culturally Relevant Teaching Strategies.* Thousand Oaks, CA: Corwin Press.

Diversity in Mathematics Education Center for Learning and Teaching (DMECLT). 2007. "Culture, Race, Power, and Mathematics Education." In *Second Handbook of Research on Mathematics Teaching and Learning,* edited by Frank K. Lester, Jr., 405–33. Charlotte, NC: Information Age.

Joseph, George Gheverghese. 1993. "A Rationale for a Multicultural Approach to Mathematics." In *Multicultural Mathematics: Teaching Mathematics from a Global Perspective,* edited by David Nelson, George Gheverghese Joseph, and Julian Williams, 1–24. Oxford, England: Oxford University Press.

Ladson-Billings, Gloria. 1994. *The Dreamkeepers: Successful Teachers of African American Children.* San Francisco: Jossey-Bass Publishers.

———. 1995. "Making Mathematics Meaningful in a Multicultural Context." In *New Directions for Equity in Mathematics Education,* edited by Walter G. Secada, Elizabeth Fennema, and Lisa B. Adajian, 126–45. New York: Cambridge University Press.

Presmeg, Norma. 2007. "The Role of Culture in Teaching and Learning Mathematics." In *Second Handbook of Research on Mathematics Teaching and Learning,* edited by Frank K. Lester, Jr., 435–58. Charlotte, NC: Information Age.

Shirley, Lawrence. 1995. "Using Ethnomathematics to Find Multicultural Mathematical Connections." In *Connecting Mathematics Across the Curriculum,* edited by Peggy A. House and Arthur F. Coxford, 34–43. Reston, VA: National Council of Teachers of Mathematics.

Smith, Margaret S., and Edward A. Silver. 1995. "Meeting the Challenges of Diversity and Relevance." *Mathematics Teaching in the Middle School* 1 (September–October): 442–48.

Tate, William F. 1995. "Mathematics Communication: Creating Opportunities to Learn." *Teaching Children Mathematics* 1 (February): 344–49, 369.

Wiest, Lynda R. 2001. "Teaching Mathematics from a Multicultural Perspective." *Equity and Excellence in Education* 34 (April): 16–25.

Zaslavsky, Claudia. 1996. *The Multicultural Math Classroom: Bringing in the World.* Portsmouth, NH: Heinemann.

CHAPTER 2

How to Select Culturally Based Media

In this chapter, we describe procedures for selecting and using resources shared in the remaining chapters of this book. Our process may be useful as you select other culturally based media resources as part of establishing culturally relevant mathematics instruction. In our selection of media, we use both a *cultural index* and a *mathematics index*. The *cultural index* indicates the extent to which the specific culture is essential to understand the message embodied in the media; the *mathematics index* indicates the extent to which mathematics is evident in the media resource. Classroom time is extremely valuable; teachers make decisions daily about the tasks they use with students and the time students need to engage in those tasks. Both the cultural index and the mathematics index are helpful to inform decisions when selecting media resources. We describe these two indexes in more detail in the following sections and raise some important issues for teachers to consider when using these resources.

Our Cultural Index

Our cultural index categorizes resources in one of three ways and is a modification of an index we first discussed in Chappell and Thompson (2000). Identified here as the A-B-C index, it classifies a resource as culturally amenable (*A*), culturally beneficial (*B*), or culturally compelling (*C*), depending on the extent to which culture is essential to the underlying story.

We use category *A*, for a *culturally amenable* resource, when the message in the resource is not dependent on the cultural (e.g., racial, ethnic) identity of the main characters in the resource. That is, "the characters portrayed could be of any race or ethnic persuasion without changing the message" conveyed through the media resource (Chappell and Thompson 2000, 135). The message within the resource suits many cultural groups, not just the majority cultural group represented in the resource. For instance, although the film *The Way Home* is set in Korea, the message of a young boy staying with his grandmother in the country and learning how to interact with her could apply to any culture or group; the message is not dependent on Korean culture although viewing the film does give students some insight into Korean country life.

Our second category, *B* for a *culturally beneficial* resource, is used when the cultural (e.g., racial, ethnic) identity of the main characters is not essential to the underlying message in the resource but the use of such persons uniquely shapes the message as well as one's response to it. Although the message resonates across cultures, the message is impacted by the context surrounding the cultural group. For instance, we classify the film *The Pursuit of Happyness* as culturally beneficial because individuals from many cultures face struggles making ends meet and trying to achieve a better life; the fact that the main character is African American raises particular challenges to succeeding in the corporate world.

Our last category, *C*, identifies a *culturally compelling* resource. Here, the cultural (e.g., racial, ethnic) identity of the main characters is essential to the message that is presented in the resource. The message depends on the cultural identity; if the culture were removed or changed, the message in the resource would be fundamentally different. We classify the film *Rabbit-Proof Fence* as culturally compelling; set in Australia, the film depicts a particular scenario of aboriginal life in the 1930s. Without the cultural context, the film lacks meaning.

Our Mathematics Index

Our mathematics index identifies two categories, depending on the extent to which mathematics is explicit (*E*) or implicit (*I*) in the resource. In some resources, mathematics content is overtly evident, illustrated, and/or mentioned in the resource. For instance, in the film *A Raisin in the Sun* (see the CD-ROM), there is explicit discussion among the family members about how to spend a $10,000 insurance check. In most resources, however, mathematics is implicit or we use the context as a springboard for mathematics investigations. Although mention is made of weaving a loom in the film *The Lost Child*, no mathematics of weaving is discussed; however, we use this context for several mathematics investigations.

Although some children's books are explicitly written to introduce mathematics concepts, most film resources are not created with a bent toward mathematics or toward any specific discipline for that matter. So, we have categorized most film resources on the mathematics index as *implicit*. However, when a resource was classified as mathematically explicit, we were careful to create an investigation that treated the mathematics content in a substantive manner and to connect the investigation back to the resource. For instance, in the film *No More Baths*, there is explicit reference to purchasing shares of the Glenwood Springs Kids' Corporation; we built an investigation related to the cost of these shares.

Table 1 summarizes the categories for both the cultural index and the mathematics index. For each resource, we include a similar table and our classifications of the resource

Table 1. Cultural and Mathematics Index Categories

Cultural Index			Mathematics Index	
Amenable	**B**eneficial	**C**ompelling	**E**xplicit	**I**mplicit
Message . . .			Content . . .	
is independent of cultural identity	is influenced by cultural identity	is dependent on cultural identity	is evident in varying degrees	varies from indirect to none

on both of these indexes. Although you may disagree with our classifications, the indexes reveal our perspective on the cultural and mathematical potential of the resource.

About the Films Media Resources

Featured in this resource are ten films in which the main and/or supporting characters have a racial or ethnic cultural identity other than Caucasian. In particular, we have chosen resources that feature characters whose cultural backgrounds are African and African American, Native American and Indigenous Peoples, Latino, or Asian and Pacific Islanders. The films are unique in many ways. Some are set in the United States; others are foreign films. Most have youth or young adolescents as main or supporting characters; for those that do not, children still have a real presence in the film. Many of the ten films are regarded as family-oriented films made specifically as television movies (e.g., the Hallmark collection); others have been feature attractions at theatres. The films are either unrated (e.g., foreign films or Hallmark Hall of Fame films) or have ratings from the Motion Picture Association of America (MPAA) no higher than PG-13.

Chapters 3–12 focus on investigations created from screenplays or television movies that highlight one of the four cultural groups previously mentioned. The investigations were designed to encompass multiple content ideas so that middle-grades students have ample opportunities to study a range of mathematics content in a culturally relevant learning environment. Although we believe there is a place for using films in the classroom, there are several issues that teachers need to consider. We address these issues in the next sections.

Factors to Consider When Using Films

Films pose some special challenges that other media resources do not. As we explored potential film resources, it became quite evident that we would have to establish a baseline for permissible content in order to feel comfortable showing the film in a middle-grades classroom. Films that went beyond our baseline were excluded from further consideration.

Most American films have a MPAA rating scale (e.g., G, PG, or PG-13), which helps individuals (especially parents or guardians) gauge whether their children should view a particular film. In contrast, many foreign films do not have a rating scale. This can make selecting films that depict groups from different cultural backgrounds an arduous task. For example, we viewed many a film that contained a great message, but its content did not seem appropriate for middle-grades students to view, at least in a public or private school classroom. Thus, we established a few criteria that served as our baseline for including a film as a possible resource from which investigations would be developed. These criteria include:

- little to no profane language;
- no sexually explicit content;
- minimal violence; and
- no extremely sensitive content.

Films that "crossed the line" for any of these criteria were deemed by us as not acceptable film resources for middle-grades students. One could argue that every such resource contains some content that might be viewed as offensive or sensitive from someone's perspective. We also know that many middle-grades students do watch films that contain blatant and charged content related to our criteria. Yet, we took into account what kinds of activity should occur on school grounds, rather than at home or in personal settings outside of school. As a teacher, you have to set criteria for your students based on school and community standards in order to decide what you should and should not use in your class.

Most foreign films contain subtitles in English. We did not necessarily exclude a film just because it had subtitles. However, we tried to be sensitive to the amount of subtitles and the speed with which they occurred. We realize that many middle-grades students are not fast readers. If we had difficulty keeping up with reading the subtitles, we assumed that middle-grades students would as well and generally excluded the film from further consideration.

A Caveat for Teachers

Regarding film resources, we strongly encourage teachers to preview all films prior to including them as part of instruction. Plainly stated, *never use a film resource with your students until you first view it yourself!* You are most familiar with the backgrounds of your students as well as the different social and cultural mores and norms of the community. Because the film resources are significant aspects of the investigations, you will want to be familiar with all aspects of the resources as part of your normal planning and preparation for any mathematics investigation, just as you would for any other mathematics investigation conducted in your classroom. You could begin by reading a review of the film, often through a World Wide Web search. The review typically provides ample information to know whether you want to preview it further. In some situations, a single inappropriate word would be unacceptable; in others, a few mildly inappropriate words would not disqualify a film from use. Some films originally shown in a theatre are eventually shown on family television and cleaned of any language or sexually explicit scenes. Some devices remove commercials and problematic episodes, and teachers might apply these devices to a film before showing it in class.

As part of your preparation, you should also check very closely the policies of your district and school pertaining to the types of films that can be viewed in class. Policies vary from school to school, and checking them before viewing a film might save you time and energy, as well as avert any potential problems. For example, school libraries may contain a select collection of film titles and a teacher may only be able to exhibit films from this collection.

Teachers do need to observe copyright regulations when viewing films with their students. Many films rented from outside sources contain notices indicating they are only to be viewed in a home entertainment environment. Schools need permission, often through district film licenses, to show such films in a typical class setting. Teachers should check all appropriate policies and, if uncertain, ask school administrators for permission before viewing films with their students.

Options for Viewing Films

Once permissions are cleared and you have previewed the film, you are ready to consider different ways to implement the resource prior to having students engage in the investigations. We offer several suggestions for using these longer film resources:

- *Classroom viewing*: A film can be viewed by students during class time. Even though this is perhaps the most convenient option, you will need to think carefully about viewing a film in class because many films can last well beyond one regular class period. You will want to plan and weigh whether classroom viewing is a viable option for prepping the class for the mathematics investigations that are to follow.

- *Homework viewing*: A second option is for students to view a film as an outside class assignment. This may mean that students are responsible for renting the film, which might be the most difficult option. However, middle-grades students are fairly accustomed to renting and viewing films, and their parents/guardians should be informed ahead of time about this assignment. Teachers should be sensitive to situations in which students do not have finances for renting a film. Many public libraries rent films at no cost. So, teachers might check the policies at libraries in their local communities.

- *Scene-selection viewing*: A third option is for students to view only specific clips of the film. This is possible as most films have scene selection options. After previewing the film, you could go directly to the scene selections and show a brief clip after providing students with an overview of the film's plot or subject matter.

- *Special-project viewing*: Yet another option is for students to view a film as part of an outside class project that a teacher might assign. The film is viewed independently by a student or a group of students, who then work on the investigations outside class.

- *Interdisciplinary viewing*: Many middle schools employ a team approach in which a group of teachers from different disciplines all teach the same group of students. Such teams often teach one or more interdisciplinary or thematic units during the year. In this scenario, students could view the film, perhaps in their English or social studies class, and then do the investigations in their mathematics class. Of course, careful and collaborative planning on the part of the teachers is imperative for students to receive maximum benefits in terms of learning outcomes.

About the Print Literature Media Resources

Fewer issues arise from the use of printed literature resources. We have primarily chosen children's literature books that we believe are appropriate for students in multiple grades. Many books, even if written for upper-elementary children, contain mathematical content well beyond elementary school mathematics. So, we consider less the suggested age range provided by the book publisher; rather, we use our own judgment about the appropriateness of the book's leading characters, the story line, and the illustrations for middle-grades students. If we believe the book is appropriate, we use it. Our experience in classrooms has led us to believe that "Every child likes a good story!" Hence, to a large extent, a children's book can be used in any grade regardless of the "reading readiness" grade level noted on the book by the publisher.

We have also chosen children's books rather than adolescent literature because children's books can be read in class in a relatively short period of time so that students can work on a mathematics investigation. Generally, we read the books aloud rather than have students read them. We can typically read children's books in less than fifteen minutes, which makes them ideal tools for teachers to use as part of culturally relevant instruction.

As with the film resources, we have selected printed literature resources that feature Africans and African Americans, Native Americans and Indigenous Peoples, Latinos, and Asians and Pacific Islanders as the main characters. We provide investigations for eighteen books, most of which teachers should find easily through their school library, district resource center, local bookstore, or online.

Factors to Consider When Using Print Literature Books

There are few special factors to consider about the print literature books. Teachers should always check their district list of books and be certain that they can read or assign to their class the books featured in our selection.

Some teachers are concerned about using children's books with middle-grades students. Personally, we have encountered no problems with this. We do believe that the books we use provide springboards for good mathematics appropriate for the middle-grades level. Teachers who may think that such books are not appropriate for use are probably better off not using them, because students will sense teachers' concerns. However, if you have not previously used such resources with your students, we encourage you to have an open mind. We have witnessed many "converts" once teachers experience using children's books with their students.

Typically, we read an entire story in class before beginning a mathematics investigation. At times, however, we might read only a portion of a story if reading the entire book would detract from students' explorations or give too many clues to the investigation. Teachers know their students and can determine the best course of action to use with a given book and given investigation.

Middle-grades teachers who use learning centers may want to make these books available for students to read again in the learning center. Some students will find a favorite story that they want to read again and again.

About the Internet Resources

Additional resources used in this book include websites that contain cultural artifacts, such as masks, flags, or games from around the world. The websites that we reference and from which we build investigations should be fairly accessible to students and teachers; this accessibility makes it possible to explore resources much more easily than in the past. Each of these Internet resources encompasses multiple cultures.

Teachers will need to check their school and district policies about accessing such websites from schools. Because of so much objectionable content on the Web, many schools block students and teachers from exploring websites. Teachers may need to work with their Web administrator to gain access to these sites or to download necessary material for use prior to classroom instruction.

Other Avenues for Identifying Culturally Based Media Resources

As you embark on a journey to incorporate culturally based resources into your classroom, we offer a few additional tips for identifying resources appropriate for use:

- Visit museums, especially those featuring cultural collections or exhibits.
- Read reviews of films from websites that tend to provide more detail than those typically found in newspapers.
- Talk to employees in film rental stores or bookstores for suggestions about resources with a cultural perspective.
- Ask colleagues from other racial or ethnic backgrounds about recommendations for good resources.

Concluding Thoughts

We close this chapter by reiterating a point made earlier. As with planning any lesson for your class, it is crucial that you preview films, preread books, and explore websites that might be used in any classroom investigations. Make certain you are comfortable with any resource before exposing your students to it. In addition, make sure that you examine any state, district, or school policies to determine how an investigation fits within the curriculum. Students can benefit tremendously from engaging in investigations generated from culturally based media resources. Nevertheless, like all supplementary resources, they must be used with purposeful intent.

References

A Raisin in the Sun. 1961. Produced by David Susskind and Philip Rose. Directed by Daniel Petric. Written by Lorraine Hansberry. 128 minutes. Columbia Pictures. Videocassette.

Chappell, Michaele F., and Denisse R. Thompson. 2000. "Fostering Multicultural Connections in Mathematics through Media." In *Changing the Faces of Mathematics: Perspectives on African Americans*, edited by Marilyn Strutchens, Martin Johnson, and William Tate, 135-50. Reston, VA: National Council of Teachers of Mathematics.

No More Baths. 2003. Produced by Rick V. Larsen and Jeff T. Miller. Written and Directed by Timothy J. Nelson. 93 minutes. Feature Films for Families. Film.

Rabbit-Proof Fence. 2002. Produced by Philip Noyce and Christine Olson. Directed by Philip Noyce. 94 minutes. Miramax Films. Film.

The Lost Child. 2000. Produced by Richard Welsh. Directed by Karen Arthur and Teleplay by Sally Beth Robinson. 98 minutes. Hallmark Hall of Fame Productions. Film.

The Pursuit of Happyness. 2006. Produced by Todd Black, Jason Blumenthal, Steve Tisch, James Lassiter, and Will Smith. Directed by Gabriele Muccino. 117 minutes. Columbia Pictures. Film.

The Way Home. 2002. Produced by Jae-woo Hang and Woo-hyun Hang. Written and Directed by Jeong-Hyang Lee. 80 minutes. CJ Entertainment. Film.

Film Resources

This section contains thirty investigations based on ten films from four cultures: nine investigations from three films featuring African American culture, eight investigations from three films featuring Native American or Indigenous Peoples cultures, six investigations from two films featuring Latino cultures, and seven investigations from two films featuring Asian cultures. The investigations span the range of the five content foci recommended in the *Principles and Standards for School Mathematics* of the National Council of Teachers of Mathematics (2000).

The majority of the investigations can be completed independent of each other, so students can work on only one investigation from a particular media. Some of the investigations are easily completed in a single class period; others are more appropriate for a multiday lesson or a longer, outside-class project. The matrix, Investigations by Content and Culture, on pages xii–xiii, cross-references all the investigations by content themes; the table that follows contains only the investigations for the film resources. All the investigations are provided on the accompanying CD-ROM.

Reference

National Council of Teachers of Mathematics. 2000. *Principles and Standards for School Mathematics.* Reston, VA: National Council of Teachers of Mathematics.

Film Investigations by Content and Culture

Resource	Number & Operations	Algebraic Thinking	Geometry	Measurement	Data Analysis & Probability
African and African American					
Akeelah and the Bee	• Learning New Words	• Learning New Words			• The Luck of the Draw • More About Spelling Bees
No More Baths	• Share Buying • Playground Design	• Share Buying	• Playground Design	• Playground Design	
The Pursuit of Happyness	• Getting Rid of the Machines • Making Cold Calls	• Getting Rid of the Machines			• Numbers in Your Head • Solving the Rubik's Cube
Native American and Indigenous Peoples					
The Lost Child	• Weaving on the Loom • Dyeing Wool	• Weaving on the Loom	• Rug Design	• Weaving on the Loom	
Rabbit-Proof Fence	• A Really Long Fence	• Walking a Long Distance	• A Really Long Fence	• A Really Long Fence • Walking a Long Distance	
Spirit of the Animals	• Whales and More Whales • An Eagle Success Story			• Whales and More Whales • Eagle Essentials	• Whales and More Whales • An Eagle Success Story
Latino					
Selena	• Are You in My Space? • Start Up That Band!	• Start Up That Band! • Fashionable Fashions	• Fashionable Fashions	• Are You in My Space?	• Are You in My Space?
Under the Same Moon	• Tomatoes, Tomatoes, Tomatoes • Taking a Trip	• Do You Have Enough Money?		• Tomatoes, Tomatoes, Tomatoes	
Asian and Pacific Islanders					
Children of Heaven	• Lavash Bread			• Lavash Bread • Winning a Place in the Race	• Shoes, Shoes, and More Shoes
The Way Home	• A Day at the Market	• A Day at the Market	• Giving Directions	• Backpacking with Shoulder Poles	• Hang Dry

CHAPTER 3

Akeelah and the Bee

About the Resource

Akeelah is a young African American girl in an inner-city environment who loves words and is adept at spelling. With coercion from her principal, she enters a school spelling contest and wins. Despite numerous obstacles in her path, she progresses through regional and state competitions on her way to a spot at the Scripps National Spelling Bee Championship. Along the way, she is encouraged by a former English professor, Dr. Larabee, who coaches her on the structure and origins of words. He challenges Akeelah to believe she can become a spelling champion. Her story shows the power of perseverance and the difference one person can make in the life of a community; her story also illustrates how one can succeed while caring about the welfare of others.

Cultural Index			Mathematics Index	
Amenable	**B**eneficial	**C**ompelling	**E**xplicit	**I**mplicit
	✓			✓

Cultural Group: African and African American

Length: 112 minutes

Rating: PG

Mathematical Focus

 Investigation: The Luck of the Draw

- probability
- simulations
- creating tree diagrams for probability

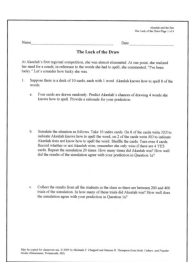

Investigation: Learning New Words

- number sense
- writing, evaluating, and solving equations
- graphing and comparing linear equations

 ## Investigation: More About Spelling Bees

- graphing data displays
- mathematical communication

Commentary About the Investigations

The first two investigations that follow are closely connected to ideas generated from the film, but are independent of each other. Students will need to have a deck of cards available for The Luck of the Draw. The investigation More About Spelling Bees is an open-ended project.

The Luck of the Draw

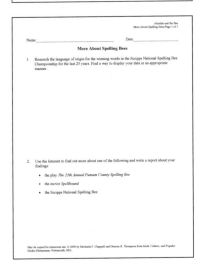

In the film, Akeelah did not initially believe that she needed a coach. When she went to the first county spelling bee, she was almost eliminated from the competition and won only because another contestant was disqualified. She commented to Javier, a contestant who befriended her, that she was lucky in her draw of words; she could easily have gotten words she did not know.

Question 1 engages students in a simulation of a probability experiment. Students can make a deck of 10 cards, with a given number representing words whose spelling is known and the others representing words whose spelling is unknown. Alternatively, a regular deck of cards can be used with specific cards (e.g., jokers or face cards) representing words whose spellings are unknown. Students simulate the competition by drawing 4 cards to represent 4 rounds of spelling and then repeat for 20 trials; for such a small number of trials, results may vary considerably. When all the students pool their data, the large number of trials should begin to approximate the theoretical probability of the result.

In Questions 2 and 3, students explore the probability symbolically as well as by constructing a tree diagram containing the probabilities along each branch. Students might construct the branches, even when there is a NO along the branch. Notice, however, that once 2 NOs have been obtained, no further branches can be constructed with a NO. For 2 unknown words among 10 cards, students have only a 33% probability of having 4 cards drawn randomly that they know how to spell.

Learning New Words

Questions 1 and 2 help students think about large numbers within an algebraic context. To learn 5,000 words in a 3-month time period (the focus of Question 1), students need to learn about 55 new words per day. This number is likely unrealistic for many students if they are studying for mastery, particularly if students need to learn the spelling, definition, parts of speech, and language of origin of the word. Question 2c focuses on learning the entire consolidated word list of 23,000 words, which many spelling bee contestants apparently do. In the question, students use a moderately easy word rate per day, so that it would take slightly more than 6 years to learn the entire list. To learn the words in a year, one needs to learn over 1,900 words per month, or over 60 words per day (Question 2d). Learning all the words in an unabridged dictionary could easily take one's entire childhood, and beyond. Thinking about the number of words can help students begin to appreciate the relative size of numbers.

Questions 3 and 4 provide students an opportunity to graph several linear equations and compare graphs. The graphs should be drawn as discrete rather than continuous graphs, because both days and words need to be whole numbers; although one could argue that fractions of days are possible, one does not learn fractions of words. The graphs for Preston and Syril are parallel, having different y-intercepts.

If students have access to graphing calculators, they might graph the equations for Cassandra, Russell, and Syril (Question 3c) using this technology. They could also graph the equation for Preston (Question 4b) on the calculator. Students could be encouraged to vary the rate of learning words and observe how the graphs of the equations change.

More About Spelling Bees

Over the last few years, the spelling bee has become an important media event with plays and movies written about the phenomenon. Contestants have coaches and train with the same diligence exhibited by top athletes. Having students investigate more information about spelling bees on the Internet provides an opportunity for students to explore specific aspects of interest to them.

Reference

Akeelah and the Bee. 2006. Produced by Nancy Hult Ganis, Sid Ganis, Laurence Fishburne, Michael Romerse, and Danny Llewelyn. Written and Directed by Doug Atchison. 112 minutes. Lionsgate. Film.

CHAPTER 4

No More Baths

About the Resource

This film features a young Caucasian boy, Keagan McPhie, who exercises both leadership and character skills as the leader of an organized kids' corporation. Keagan is quite fond of his aging African American neighbor, Jake Brewing, who is threatened by an aggressive developer with plans to acquire Jake's real-estate property for future development. Keagan leads the corporation in a peaceful protest to take no more baths until something is done to help Jake. The film depicts how individuals—adults and children alike—can assume their civic responsibilities, join together to solve their differences, and make their communities better places to live.

Cultural Index			Mathematics Index	
Amenable	**Beneficial**	**Compelling**	**Explicit**	**Implicit**
	✓		✓	

Cultural Group: African and African American

Length: 93 minutes

Rating: Not rated (Feature Films for Families)

Mathematical Focus

 Investigation: Share Buying

- number sense
- writing and evaluating algebraic expressions
- solving inequalities

No More Baths
Share Buying/Page 1 of 2

Name_____ Date_____

Share Buying

At some point in the past, Jake Brewing had deeded 1 acre of his real-estate property to the Glenwood Springs Kids Corporation, Inc. In order to raise enough funds to pay Jake's real-estate taxes and bring his house up to code, the corporation agreed to sell its acre in one-hundredth portion shares.

1. Keagan's parents were the first to request 2 one-hundredth portion shares of the acre for $5,000. Determine the amount they paid per one-hundredth portion share.

2. a. Several other individuals purchased multiple shares of the acre. Using the cost per one-hundredth share you found in Question 1, what is the amount of money collected when 5 one-hundredth shares are sold? 10 one-hundredth shares? 35 one-hundredth shares?

   b. Write an expression that represents the amount of money collected when s one-hundredth shares are sold.

3. According to the court testimony, Jake needed $147,000 to pay hiss property taxes and to bring his house up to building code. What expression represents how much more money was needed after s shares were sold?

May be copied for classroom use. © 2009 by Michaele F. Chappell and Denisse R. Thompson from *Math, Culture, and Popular Media* (Heinemann: Portsmouth, NH).

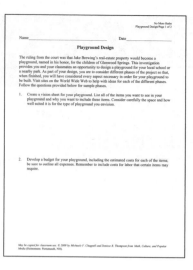

Investigation: Playground Design

- problem solving
- geometry and measurement
- financial budgeting

Commentary About the Investigations

These investigations are independent of each other. In particular, Playground Design is likely a multiday lesson and, if expanded, could be an ideal project for a school-community partnership.

Share Buying

The Share Buying investigation builds off the court trial that occurs near the end of the film when the judge rules that Jake Brewing has 1 month to raise monies to pay his real-estate taxes and bring his house up to building code. Beginning with Keagan's parents, persons in the courtroom yell out shares per hundredth that they would be willing to purchase to help Jake raise his funds. Initially, Keagan's dad announces that he will pay $2,000 for a one-hundredth share of the acre; then the mom immediately amends that offer, making it $5,000 for 2 shares of the acre. Thus in Question 1, the investigation begins with a basic number calculation requiring students to determine the amount paid per one-hundredth share from the latter offer. Teachers should check that students have the correct cost for a one-hundredth share before attempting the remaining questions.

In Questions 2 and 3, students think more generally about how to represent the purchased share amounts. For example, in comical courtroom frenzy, several individuals call out different amounts of shares they wish to purchase. In Question 2b, students represent the amount algebraically after s shares are purchased. Because a specific total that Jake needs is mentioned at the trial, in Question 3 students write an algebraic expression representing the remaining funds needed to meet this total after s shares are purchased.

Question 4 takes into account the total monies raised from the sale of shares. Because more was raised than needed in the situation, students must determine an inequality that represents the maximum number of shares sold. Afterward, they can solve the inequality to determine how many one-hundredth shares were sold. Note that this is a situation in which students must round *down* to the nearest integer. They could then discuss the meaning of partial shares and what that means for this scenario.

Playground Design

In this investigation, students engage in an open-ended project to plan and design a playground for their local school or a nearby park within their community. This task builds off the ruling made in the film that Jake Brewing's real-estate property would become a playground, named in his honor, for the children of Glenwood Springs. Students work in pairs or small groups to complete this potentially multiday project.

This investigation offers four directives to guide students' work and help them get started on each phase. Students conduct their research, discuss ideas, and finalize their decisions; so, they need ample time to complete the project and prepare their research for presentation. Students will engage in a substantial amount of problem solving while working on this task. Once they plan the type of playground desired, they should use grid paper or an electronic drawing tool to generate a blueprint of their playground, placing, for example, the arrangement of different equipment, walking spaces, or greenery in the layout. Students apply geometry and measurement skills as they carry out the task. Then, students devise a budget for their playground, including possibilities for obtaining the income through fund-raising events to cover the expenses they will incur for equipment, labor, and delivery.

Several options can be introduced to students at the different phases of the investigation. For example, students could collect catalogs from playground vendors to determine type and cost of equipment. They certainly should conduct some of their research using the Internet to learn of different options available when planning their playgrounds. For example, students might desire to build an environmentally safe playground, which may call for special equipment to be made from certain types of materials. Teachers should explore potential websites prior to assigning this investigation. Some useful and student-friendly websites are listed.

www.peacefulplaygrounds.com
www.dreamplaygrounds.co.uk
www.world-playground.com

Reference

No More Baths. 2003. Produced by Rick V. Larsen and Jeff T. Miller. Written and Directed by Timothy J. Nelson. 93 minutes. Feature Films for Families. Film.

CHAPTER 5

The Pursuit of Happyness

About the Resource

This film is inspired by the true story of Chris Gardner, an African American man who literally went from "rags to riches" by working on Wall Street. In the film, he is a salesman struggling to make ends meet by selling portable bone density scanners to doctors in the San Francisco Bay area. He raises his five-year-old son as a single father while taking advantage of an opportunity to participate in an unpaid, highly competitive broker-training program; only one of twenty interns will be selected for a position in the company at the end of the program. With little to no income, Chris and his son are evicted from his apartment and an extended-stay hotel, and they are forced to sleep in homeless shelters and in the men's public restroom of the city transportation station. However, with strong determination and confidence, as well as the love of his son, Chris triumphs over these obstacles to become famous on Wall Street.

Cultural Index			Mathematics Index	
Amenable	Beneficial	Compelling	Explicit	Implicit
	✓		✓	

Cultural Group: African and African American

Length: 117 minutes

Rating: PG-13

Mathematical Focus

 Investigation: Getting Rid of the Machines

- number sense
- average costs
- writing and graphing linear equations, including piecewise linear equations

The Pursuit of Happyness
Getting Rid of the Machines/Page 1 of 3

Name _____ Date _____

Getting Rid of the Machines

In the film, Chris sells portable bone density scanner machines. He invested all of his savings to purchase approximately 40 of these scanners to sell to local doctors.

1. In the film, it is not clear how much Chris originally charged for the machines. Early in the film, one doctor did not buy a machine, commenting that the cost was too high.

    a. Suppose Chris originally charged $750 for the machines. If he sold 15 machines at this cost, how much did he earn from the sales of these 15 machines?

    b. What percent of the machines did he sell for $750?

    c. Later in the film, Chris needed to sell the machines to have money for rent. There is a scene in the film in which a doctor writes a check for $250 when he buys a machine. How much did Chris earn from the sales of the remaining machines at $250 each? (Remember that Chris already sold 15 machines at a higher price.)

    d. Combine your results from Questions 1a and 1c to find the total amount Chris earned if he sold all the machines at the amounts given in these questions.

May be copied for classroom use. © 2009 by Michaele F. Chappell and Denisse R. Thompson from *Math, Culture, and Popular Media* (Heinemann: Portsmouth, NH).

Investigation: Making Cold Calls

- number sense
- percents
- problem solving

 Investigation: Numbers in Your Head

- data analysis
- measures of center
- graphical displays

 Investigation: Solving the Rubik's Cube

- data analysis
- problem solving

Commentary About the Investigations

These investigations all relate to scenes from the film and can be completed independent of each other. For Numbers in Your Head and Solving the Rubik's Cube, students will need access to stopwatches or some other time-keeping device. Teachers should have a Rubik's Cube model available for Solving the Rubik's Cube.

Getting Rid of the Machines

This investigation builds on the major plot in the film, namely Chris' attempts to sell the bone density machines. The original price for the machines is not provided in the film; later it appears that Chris lowered the price to sell machines for rent money. So, a possible sale price is created at the beginning for the purposes of exploration (Question 1).

Although students may have had some experience with graphing linear equations, they may not have had prior experience with graphing piecewise linear equations (Question 3), that is, equations defined differently over different domains. The word *domain* is not used in the investigation, but students should be able to consider which values of the independent variable are appropriate for each equation based on the sale cost. When students graph each equation, they should not connect the points; the situation is discrete because one cannot sell part of a machine.

In Question 4, students have an opportunity to consider reasonable costs for the machines given the expected sale cost. Students should realize that a profit is made when the money from sales is greater than the original costs; a loss occurs when the money from sales is smaller than the original costs; an individual breaks even when the money from sales equals the money from costs. The problem is open-ended because specific information about the original cost Chris paid is not provided. Rather, students need to determine a reasonable cost given specific constraints.

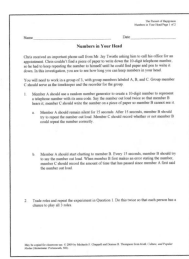

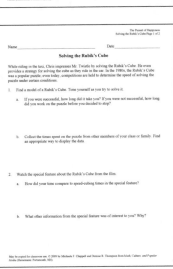

Making Cold Calls

In this investigation, students investigate the numbers of customers and their monthly deposits in order for Chris to collect the minimum amount required to meet the brokerage company's goals. Many students may have experienced telemarketers, salespeople, or fund-raisers calling their home to get them to buy something or make a contribution. You might survey students to collect data about how often they or their parents have responded positively to such phone calls. This type of survey might help students understand the concept of *cold calls* (Question 1). The number of customers obtained from those cold calls (Question 2b) is used as a basis for later questions, so teachers may want to ensure that students have a correct solution to this question before proceeding further. Many students may be surprised that the percent of calls yielding customers is only 4% when they started with 20%; however, students should realize that 20% of 20% is 4%.

In Question 4, students need to think about the total number of deposits made by the 128 customers Chris obtains each month. The customers obtained in the first month make 6 deposits each; those obtained in the last month make only 1 deposit. Question 4a provides an opportunity for students to investigate multiple strategies to obtain the total value of deposits in an efficient manner. Although brute force results in

$$128 \bullet 1,500 \bullet 6 + 128 \bullet 1,500 \bullet 5 + 128 \bullet 1,500 \bullet 4 + 128 \bullet 1,500 \bullet 3 + 128 \bullet 1,500 \bullet 2 + 128 \bullet 1,500,$$

the use of algebraic properties facilitates a more efficient solution,

$$128 \bullet 1,500 \bullet (6 + 5 + 4 + 3 + 2 + 1).$$

In Question 4b, students will need to think about the total number of deposits made over 6 months, namely $128 \bullet (6 + 5 + 4 + 3 + 2 + 1)$, and use this number to determine a reasonable value for the average deposit.

Question 5 is a nonroutine problem. There are many possible solutions, depending on the number of customers in a given month. Chris might obtain a lot of customers in the first month and have them make $1,000 deposits for each of 6 months; or, he might have more customers in later months. The longer customers make deposits, the fewer customers Chris will need to reach his goals. If students have access to a spreadsheet, teachers might encourage them to explore different scenarios for the number of customers by month and the total of their deposits using a spreadsheet.

Numbers in Your Head

This investigation should be of interest to students because they are collecting data about themselves, namely their ability to remember a string of unrelated numbers. Although these numbers are meant to represent a telephone number, the actual numbers are not likely to have much meaning for students. Students should work in small groups and collect data for 3 trials of the experiment; when the data for the entire class are collated, there should be at least 20–30 data values. Teachers may need to help students learn how to use a random number generator from a calculator or to use a random number table in a book.

Depending on the variability in the data, the mean or the median might be more representative; it is also possible that the mode could be introduced if the number of seconds is the same for a large number of students. If one or more students are able to remember the string of numbers for a much longer or much shorter time than other students, teachers should take the opportunity to discuss the concept of *outliers* and how outliers influence the mean much more than the median.

Solving the Rubik's Cube

The Rubik's Cube was an extremely popular puzzle in the 1980s. In this investigation, students can try to solve the puzzle and time themselves as they do so. Students may be very interested in learning that there are speed competitions for solving the cube and that some people solve the puzzle blindfolded or with one hand. This investigation is appropriate as an outside-class project for interested students. For some students, trying to solve the puzzle is likely to be frustrating.

Reference

The Pursuit of Happyness. 2006. Produced by Todd Black, Jason Blumenthal, Steve Tisch, James Lassiter, and Will Smith. Directed by Gabriele Muccino. 117 minutes. Columbia Pictures. Film.

CHAPTER 6

The Lost Child

About the Resource

In this Hallmark Hall of Fame film, a woman who had been adopted as a child searches for her biological family. She discovers that she is a native Navajo and decides to meet her biological relatives who live on a reservation out west. She takes her children to meet her family and is later joined by her Caucasian husband. The film chronicles her journey and that of her family as they learn about their Native American heritage and life on the reservation.

Cultural Index			Mathematics Index	
Amenable	**B**eneficial	**C**ompelling	**E**xplicit	**I**mplicit
		✓		✓

The film's special features are also worth viewing. Many of the Native American actors comment positively about participating in a film depicting modern Native American life.

Cultural Group: Native American and Indigenous Peoples

Length: 98 minutes

Rating: Not rated

Mathematical Focus

 Investigation: Weaving on the Loom

- problem solving
- writing algebraic expressions
- one- and two-dimensional measurement
- cost per unit area

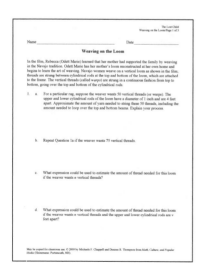

Investigation: Dyeing Wool

- ratios
- proportional reasoning
- simulations

 Investigation: Rug Design

- line symmetry

Commentary About the Investigations

These investigations are independent of each other. For Dyeing Wool, students will need small cups, water, food coloring, and cotton swabs. For Question 1 on Rug Design, students will need access to a small loom.

Weaving on the Loom

The Navajo are known for the quality of their weaving. In the film, the mother of the main character had supported her family by weaving and selling her wares. So, the daughter, Rebecca (Odett Marie), wanted to learn the weaving process. Her relatives delivered her mother's loom to the house where her husband rebuilt the loom; her aunt then taught her how to weave. This activity engages students in thinking about issues needed to weave a rug.

In Question 1–3, students estimate the amount of yarn or wool needed to form the basis of the rug. This is not a trivial task given that the loom is threaded from top to bottom and end to end in one continuous piece. Thus, students have to consider the amount of yarn needed to loop around the cylindrical rods as well as the amount of yarn needed for the vertical threads. Students are encouraged to create algebraic expressions that would estimate the amount of thread given the number of vertical threads and the distance between the cylindrical rods. Students also need to consider the amount of yarn needed and the cost, which can vary considerably depending on the type of yarn or wool that is used.

In Question 4, students consider the selling costs for rugs in terms of area. Certainly cost depends on many factors, including the reputation of the weaver and the quality of the weave. However, cost per unit area is one factor that could be considered. This task is also one in which there is no one correct answer. Students need to use data and make a rational decision based on that data; thus they are engaged in statistical reasoning. If students do further investigation of costs on the Internet, they are likely to be surprised at the range of prices and at the potential costs of the rugs. A natural extension would be to organize the costs and determine appropriate descriptive statistics (e.g., mode, median, range).

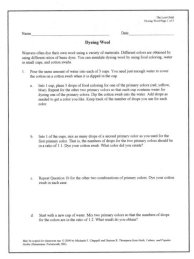

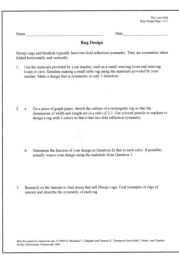

Dyeing Wool

Teachers should prepare for this activity by purchasing food coloring and collecting small containers or cups for water. For dyeing cotton swabs, cold water is fine.

Questions 1–3 simulate a science experiment as students mix primary colors in different ratios to obtain a range of colors. The three primary colors (red, yellow, and blue) can be mixed to obtain the secondary colors (red and yellow = orange, yellow and blue = green, and red and blue = violet). Between the secondary and primary colors, one obtains the tertiary colors. Students should record the ratios of the numbers of drops when mixing primary colors and the resulting color obtained.

Questions 4–6 help students develop proportional reasoning, by considering the relationship of water to drops of coloring and how the ratios of these two quantities influence the intensity of the color. If students are also taking art, mathematics teachers might work with art teachers to make an integrated unit of color and weave.

Rug Design

In this investigation, students have an opportunity to simulate weaving a rug with particular characteristics, namely one- or two-fold symmetry. Small looms, similar to those used to make pot holders with loops, are good for simulating Navajo weaving (Question 1) as in Figure 6.1. Such looms can be purchased relatively inexpensively at many

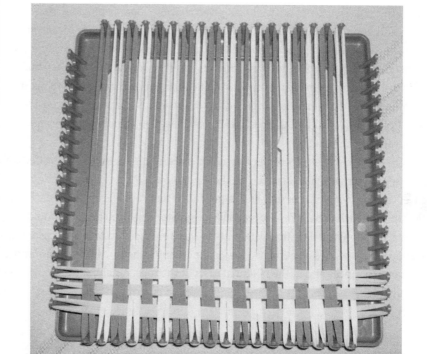

FIGURE 6.1
Loom

major outlets that sell craft supplies. By including color, the task becomes more complex because color is part of the symmetry (Question 2a). In addition, students are expected to consider what portion of the rug design is in each color, thus focusing on fractions and/or area (Question 2b).

Many Internet sites sell Navajo rugs or post pictures of rugs for sale. In Question 3, students might explore a range of sites to investigate a diversity of patterns in the rugs. Numerous sites arise from a simple Google search.

Reference

The Lost Child. 2000. Produced by Richard Welsh. Directed by Karen Arthur and Teleplay by Sally Beth Robinson. 98 minutes. Hallmark Hall of Fame Productions. Film.

CHAPTER 7

Spirit of the Animals

About the Resource

This DVD contains three short films, each about thirty minutes. In *Gift of Whales*, a young Native American boy believes that the whales have come to help him; he learns about whales from a wildlife scientist who tells him about characteristics of whales. In *Spirit of the Eagle*, a group of young students takes a trip to a wildlife camp and learns about the habits of the bald eagle. The guides are Native Americans whose tribe has a special affinity with the eagle. In *Winter Wolf*, farmers are concerned when wolves return to the public forest lands near their ranches; a biologist tries to help them understand that wolves will not harm their livestock as long as the wolves' natural food supply of elk is available. The investigations do not focus on this latter film.

Cultural Index			Mathematics Index	
Amenable	**B**eneficial	**C**ompelling	**E**xplicit	**I**mplicit
		✓	✓	

Cultural Group: Native American and Indigenous Peoples

Length: 90 minutes total, divided relatively equally among three films

Rating: Not rated (but appropriate for general audiences)

Mathematical Focus

 Investigation: Whales and More Whales

- measurement conversions
- percent, including percent decrease
- reading and interpreting data tables
- graphical displays

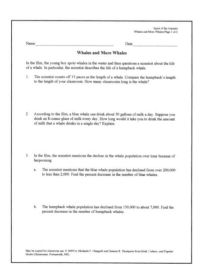

Investigation: Eagle Essentials

- measurement comparisons

 Investigation: An Eagle Success Story

- number sense, including percent increase
- data analysis and interpretation

Commentary About the Investigations

These three investigations can be completed independent of each other. In both Whales and More Whales and An Eagle Success Story, students will need access to the Internet.

Whales and More Whales

The first three questions in this investigation are based on facts provided by the scientist in the film. Students are likely to be surprised by the time it would take them to drink the amount a baby whale drinks in a single day—800 days; this time is too large for many students to comprehend unless they transform it to slightly more than 2 years.

The information about the demise of the whale population is quite startling, particularly when students realize that over 90% of the population of a specific species has disappeared. Many students view whales as majestic and are interested in ways to protect these massive creatures. The International Whaling Commission (the source of data for Question 4) sets limits on whale catches, both commercially and for aboriginal subsistence fishing. Students can explore data from this site; they may be surprised to find that some countries still continue to hunt whales for commercial purposes. Although aboriginal peoples are permitted to hunt whales to maintain their culture and lifestyle, there has been some controversy about native peoples conducting whale hunts given the diminishing numbers of whales.

Teachers might have students work in groups to collect the data for Question 5. Groups could be assigned a particular year, collecting the data and creating the graph (likely a circle graph). Different groups can then share their results with the entire class. Thus, students can construct one graph but still be able to compare graphs for multiple years.

Eagle Essentials

In this investigation, students compare eagle and human measurements. Students often hear measurements but fail to have a good feel for them. In particular, the wingspan of an eagle is greater than the height of most middle-grades students by at least 1 to 2 feet.

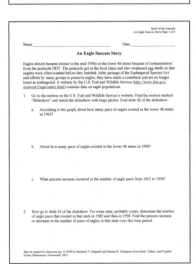

In Question 2, students need to collect data to approximate the distance an eagle can see. Although the problem is set for completion on a football field, teachers could have students attempt to read a letter on a sheet of paper from one end of a hallway to another, as long as the length of the hallway is known. To be a fair experiment, students should write the number on a sheet of paper using a dark marker that has a chance of being seen from some distance away.

It is hard to imagine an eagle's nest that might weigh 4,000 pounds, yet that is not uncommon. Because eagles mate for life, they often return to the same nest year after year, constantly adding to the nest. Over time, the nest becomes quite heavy.

An Eagle Success Story

In this investigation, students investigate data that document the return of the bald eagle in the lower forty-eight states from near extinction to a healthy population that is no longer on the endangered species list. Students are expected to investigate data that are available on a government website, namely the website of the U.S. Fish and Wildlife Service.

Questions 1c and 3b provide opportunities for students to work with percents greater than 100. Many students may be tempted to find the percent increase by finding the difference between the numbers and then finding what percent this number is of the larger number. Instead, teachers will need to help students realize that the percent increase or decrease must be made based on the relative position of the number at the beginning of the perceived change.

The slide show on the federal government website is interesting and contains many beautiful pictures of eagles in their habitats. The overall data and the data by state of the eagle population provide a means for students to track changes in a state of interest to them—likely their own state.

Reference

Spirit of the Animals. 1989. Produced by Jan C. Nickman. Written and Directed by Kathleen Phelan. 90 minutes. Miramar Images. Film.

CHAPTER 8

Rabbit-Proof Fence

About the Resource

Set in Australia, this film is based on a true story chronicled in the book *Follow the Rabbit-Proof Fence* by Doris Pilkington (1996), born as Nugi Garimara. In the 1930s, Australia had a policy of taking mixed-race Aborigines children from their homes and placing them in special residential schools for the purpose of integrating them into the majority-white society and preparing them for domestic work. Today, these children are known as the "stolen generation." When three young girls are taken from their home to the school 1,200 miles away, they soon run away and begin a long trek home.

Cultural Index			Mathematics Index	
Amenable	**B**eneficial	**C**ompelling	**E**xplicit	**I**mplicit
		✓		✓

In the early 1900s, a fence was built through a large part of Western Australia to keep rabbits from entering and destroying farmers' lands. This rabbit-proof fence becomes a guide that the girls use to lead themselves home.

Cultural Group: Native American and Indigenous Peoples

Length: 94 minutes

Rating: Not rated

Language: English with a few subtitles at the beginning of the film

Mathematical Focus

 ### Investigation: A Really Long Fence

- solving problems using rates (currency conversion)
- problem solving (drawing a sketch)
- Pythagorean Theorem

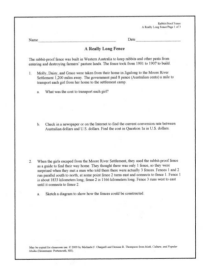

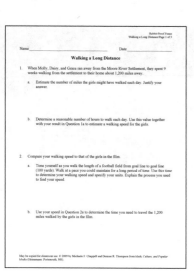

Investigation: Walking a Long Distance

- dimensional analysis
- finding speeds
- writing algebraic expressions
- graphing and solving linear equations, including systems of equations

Commentary About the Investigations

Teachers may use these two investigations as connected lessons or independent of each other. In Walking a Long Distance, students will need to collect data outside of the classroom.

A Really Long Fence

This activity uses information about the rabbit-proof fence and provides students with an opportunity to work with several mathematics concepts. For instance, in the first question, students use the given information to convert Australian currency to U.S. currency. Students can use rates or proportions; they might investigate Internet sites that convert from one currency to another.

In the second question, students first interpret a description of a situation by making a sketch, which is an important problem-solving strategy. (In the entry for Rabbit-Proof Fence in Wikipedia [http://en.wikipedia.org/wiki/Rabbit-proof_fence], there is a map showing the general orientation of the three fences.) Questions 3 through 5 provide an opportunity for students to explore the Pythagorean Theorem. Teachers should expect some slight variability in lengths for the hypotenuse (Question 3) depending on students' accuracy with measuring. However, the values that students are asked to investigate are all Pythagorean triples. Teachers need to verify that students have obtained the correct pattern for the theorem in Question 3 before they use it in Questions 4 and 5.

In both Questions 4 and 5, students might stop after finding the length of the hypotenuse. Because both questions request the distance the girls *saved* by walking the hypotenuse, the solutions are found by determining the difference between the length of the hypotenuse and the sum of the lengths of the legs. For Question 5 in particular, students might explore the distances using a spreadsheet.

Walking a Long Distance

In Questions 1 and 2, students have an opportunity to compare their walking speeds to that of the girls in the film. Students should be encouraged to use dimensional analysis to determine the walking speed of the girls as well as their own walking speed. For instance, suppose a student walks the 100 yards of the football field in 90 seconds. Then, the walking speed is:

$$\frac{100 \text{ yards}}{90 \text{ sec}} \cdot \frac{1 \text{ mi}}{1{,}760 \text{ yards}} \cdot \frac{60 \text{ sec}}{1 \text{ min}} \cdot \frac{60 \text{ min}}{1 \text{ hr}} \approx 2.3 \frac{\text{mi}}{\text{hr}}.$$

In Question 3, students use their prior work to personalize the situation to a context of their choice.

Question 4 engages students in algebraic thinking. As students complete the table, they should realize that the distance (d) from the settlement for the girls after h hours is given by the equation, $d = 2.5(6) + 2.5h$ because the girls have a 6-hour head start. For the tracker, the distance is given by $d = 3.5h$. When students graph these equations, they should realize that the tracker and the girls are the same distance from the settlement when the graphs intersect. However, students might need help in interpreting what the coordinates of the intersection mean. The y-coordinate gives the distance of the tracker and the girls from the settlement; the x-coordinate gives the number of hours the tracker has traveled whereas the girls have traveled an additional 6 hours. When the students set the 2 equations equal, they should find that the tracker will catch the girls after 15 hours.

Reference

Rabbit-Proof Fence. 2002. Produced by Philip Noyce and Christine Olson. Directed by Philip Noyce. 94 minutes. Miramax Films. Film.

CHAPTER 9

Selena

About the Resource

This film chronicles the life of Selena, a major Latina music icon in the 1990s. It documents her musical rise from the time she was a young child until she became a Grammy-winning star. Selena first achieved success as a Spanish-language artist. However, she was poised to become a crossover star into the English-language music world when she was murdered at the age of twenty-three by the president of her fan club.

Cultural Index			Mathematics Index	
Amenable	**B**eneficial	**C**ompelling	**E**xplicit	**I**mplicit
		✓		✓

Cultural Group: Latino

Length: 128 minutes

Rating: PG

Mathematical Focus

 Investigation: Are You in My Space?

- population density per square unit of area
- estimating large numbers of people
- statistical reasoning

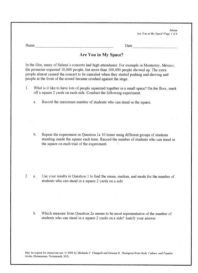

Investigation: Start Up That Band!

- percents, including percent of discount

- rates and comparisons of rates

- graphing and comparing linear equations, including systems of equations

 Investigation: Fashionable Fashions

- line symmetry

- rotational symmetry

- writing algebraic expressions for linear combinations

- graphing linear equations and finding integer solutions to the equation

Commentary About the Investigations

The three investigations in this chapter could be completed as a unit or independent of each other. Students should have access to calculator technology, preferably graphing calculators for Start Up That Band! and Fashionable Fashions.

Are You in My Space?

The questions in this activity provide students an opportunity to collect data (Question 1), determine a representative measure for the data (Question 2b), and then use that representative measure to solve additional problems (Question 2d). The work in Question 2 provides the basis for determining the square yards per person allowed in other spaces according to fire codes.

In many situations in which large crowds are present, such as concerts, tickets are collected and can be used to provide an indication of the size of the crowd. However, at other situations, such as parades or rallies, tickets are not collected; yet, officials or other individuals want to estimate the size of the crowd. So, Questions 4 and 5 focus on such situations, first by having students simulate a method to estimate the crowd and then having them investigate with local authorities about the techniques they use.

In Question 6, students are encouraged to investigate the capacities of stadiums, arenas, or other venues close to them. Students need to determine appropriate ways to display the data. For instance, high school stadiums tend to hold fewer people than college or professional stadiums. Students' graphical displays will need to accommodate large differences in the range of capacities. Another extension is to have students investigate sizes of various stadiums in the United States or abroad.

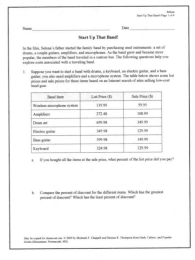

Start Up That Band!

This investigation provides opportunities for students to consider the cost of starting a band. Initially, students consider the costs for instruments similar to those purchased by Selena's father (Question 1). Students then extend this idea to determining the cost of instruments for a school instrumental ensemble (Question 2a) as well as their own band (Question 2b). There are many sites on the Internet for purchasing musical instruments.

Custom buses, such as those of many rock stars and bands, are generally quite expensive, often costing hundreds of thousands of dollars. Questions 3 and 4 provide opportunities for students to work with linear equations. In Question 3, students work with an equation of the form $y = mx + b$, where b is the fixed cost (the price of the bus) and m is the cost per mile (the cost per gallon divided by the miles per gallon). In Question 4, students compare the costs of a propane bus versus a diesel bus. Although a propane bus initially costs more, its operating costs are lower. So, at some point the difference in the initial cost is overcome. Students can determine when the two graphs intersect to determine at what point costs for the two buses are equivalent and when one bus is more economical than another.

Fashionable Fashions

The film highlights the fact that Selena was interested in fashion design as well as singing. Fashion design is big business. This activity uses the context of fashion design to engage students in explorations related to symmetry. By focusing on the design of rectangular scarves or pieces of jewelry, students can build designs that have line and/or rotational symmetry. For students who have not previously had any experiences with symmetry, teachers will likely need to provide some informal definitions. Students can create their designs on graph paper. If teachers have access to patty paper (i.e., very thin paper often placed between meat patties), students can create their designs on such paper so that they can easily fold or rotate the paper and see how designs align.

Many young designers participate in major fashion shows despite the cost, believing that the financial investment is essential to bring their designs to the attention of major buyers. Question 3 has students consider different combinations of scarves and jewelry pieces that could generate income to cover the basic cost of participating in a fashion show. If students graph by hand, they may need help considering appropriate intervals for the axes. Using the equation $120S + 80J = 100,000$, the S-axis has intercept $S = 833.3$ and the J-axis has intercept $J = 1250$. So, the S-axis might extend from 0 to 1,000 by intervals of 100 and the J-axis might extend from 0 to 1,500 by intervals of 100. If graphing calculators are available, students will need to solve the equation for one of the variables before entering it into their calculator; they could then use a table to obtain integer combinations for the numbers of scarves and jewelry designs.

Reference

Selena. 1997. Produced by Moctesuma Esparza. Written and Directed by Gregory Nava. 128 minutes. Warner Brothers. Film.

CHAPTER 10

Under the Same Moon

About the Resource

Nine-year-old Carlitos lives in Mexico with his grandmother while his mother, Rosario (an undocumented worker), works in the United States to build a better life for her family. Each Sunday, Carlitos and his mother talk via the phone at an appointed time. When the grandmother dies, Carlitos decides to travel to the United States to join his mother. This film tells of his incredible journey, adventures, and problem-solving skills as he aims to find his mother before she is scheduled to call him again.

Cultural Index			Mathematics Index	
Amenable	**B**eneficial	**C**ompelling	Explicit	Implicit
		✓		✓

Cultural Group: Latino

Length: 110 minutes

Rating: PG-13

Language: Spanish with English subtitles

Mathematics Focus

Investigation: Do You Have Enough Money?

- writing algebraic expressions
- writing, solving, and graphing algebraic equations

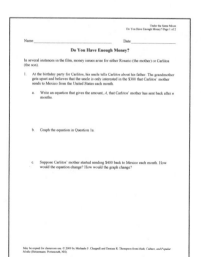

Investigation: Tomatoes, Tomatoes, Tomatoes

- working with rates
- weight measurements

 Investigation: Taking a Trip

- problem solving
- financial planning

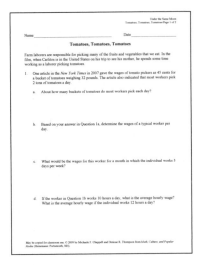

Commentary About the Investigations

The three investigations are independent of each other. Taking a Trip is an open-ended activity that is ideal for an out-of-class student project.

Do You Have Enough Money?

The tasks in this investigation focus on matters about money raised in the film. The investigation calls for students to write, graph, and solve algebraic expressions and equations.

Many Mexican workers, as well as immigrants from other countries, regularly send money to family members in their home country; this transfer of money is the focus of Question 1. Students write an equation to indicate the amount of money sent over time and then graph this linear equation. Graphing calculators would be beneficial to enable students to graph multiple equations with different coefficients of the independent variable. Students should realize that the coefficient is related to the slope of the line.

One scene in the movie suggests that Rosario sews dresses she then sells to raise money to pay a lawyer to help with her immigration status. So, Question 2 focuses on the number of dresses she needs to sew and sell to raise the necessary money. In Question 2a, students complete a table to generate a pattern in order to write an expression to represent the amount Rosario makes from sewing and selling d dresses. Notice that in Question 2b, students might write one of three equations depending on their choice of the starting point, namely the total Rosario needs for the lawyer ($4,000), the amount still to raise if she already has $2,300 (i.e., $1,700), or the amount still to raise if she already has $2,000 (i.e., $2,000). In Question 2c, students need to *round up* regardless of the decimal value because the value represents a definite number of dresses; failure to round up will leave Rosario short of the total amount of money she needs.

A natural extension, particularly if students have access to graphing calculators, is to have students graph the equations from Question 2b. Each equation is a line with negative slope; the y-intercepts correspond to the starting point for raising money.

Tomatoes, Tomatoes, Tomatoes

In areas with large populations of migrants or farm laborers, the questions raised in this investigation may be of particular interest to students. Many Mexican immigrants have often worked as migrant workers, picking fresh fruits and vegetables in U.S. fields. Recent immigration difficulties caused problems for farmers who were not able to hire enough migrants to pick their crops. In some cases, farmers chose not to plant their fields because of the lack of laborers to harvest the crops.

In certain areas of the United States, migrant workers have banded together to improve wages and working conditions in the picking of some crops, such as tomatoes used by many fast-food chains. At issue was an increase of a single penny per pound for the workers (www.nytimes.com/2007/11/29/opinion/29schlosser.html). Some fast-food chains fought against the increase.

A nice extension is to have students actually begin a small garden in the classroom and observe tomato plants as they grow. Hydroponic gardening is relatively clean as students don't need to dig in dirt. Hydroponic gardening may be the wave of the future so that individuals can be self-sufficient. In some parts of the world, this type of gardening holds real potential to feed the population because it does not require as much water as conventional farming.

Taking a Trip

Students often travel on vacations or other type trips. Classes often take culminating trips at some point during middle grades. So, this investigation helps students focus on thinking about the expenses that are incurred. After the first question, the activity is open so that students can determine where they want to travel, how they want to travel, and what meals and other needs factor into the expense. If the school student government, band, or extracurricular club regularly takes a trip during the year, teachers might encourage students to plan a trip for that group and write a report detailing information about projected costs.

Reference

Under the Same Moon. 2008. Produced by Patricia Riggen and Gerardo Barrera. Written by Ligiah Villalobos and Directed by Patricia Riggen. 110 minutes. Twentieth Century Fox. Film.

CHAPTER 11

The Way Home

About the Resource

This foreign-film classic presents a modern-day scenario of Sang-Woo, a seven-year-old privileged boy, who has major culture shock when his mother takes him from the city for an extended stay with his maternal grandmother in rural Korea. Although initially selfish and focused only on playing his video game, Sang-Woo eventually comes to appreciate Grandma's silent way of expressing her love and devotion to him.

	Cultural Index		Mathematics Index	
Amenable	**B**eneficial	**C**ompelling	Explicit	Implicit
✓				✓

Cultural Group: Asian and Pacific Islanders

Length: 80 minutes

Rating: PG

Language: Korean with English subtitles

Mathematical Focus

 ### Investigation: A Day at the Market

- number sense
- comparing costs
- proportions
- writing algebraic expressions

 ### Investigation: Hang Dry

- permutations
- combinations model of multiplication

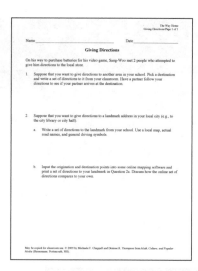

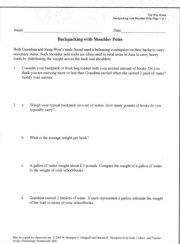

Investigation: Giving Directions

- spatial orientation
- writing and following directions

Investigation: Backpacking with Shoulder Poles

- measurement (weight)

Commentary About the Investigations

The tasks in these investigations are closely related to situations from the film. Each activity is independent of the others. Teachers will want to collect a set of maps before using Giving Directions. Many automobile-travel clubs are likely willing to provide a set of maps for school use. Teachers will need several sets of weighing scales for Backpacking with Shoulder Poles.

A Day at the Market

Prior to using the activity, teachers will want to check the Internet or a newspaper to determine the current value of the Korean won in U.S. dollars; in September 2008, the exchange rate was 1 won = $.000896 (www.seoulsearching.com/money/currency.html). So students need to compute with small numbers. In addition, teachers will want some ads showing the cost of AA batteries at several local stores. If there is an international market nearby, teachers may want to look for choco pies or some equivalent; at an international market, we found Yo' Pies, a Turkish version of the favorite Korean snack.

This activity provides an opportunity for students to engage in number work with proportions (Questions 1 and 2) as well as some algebraic thinking (Question 3). Answers to Question 3c will vary as students determine a solution based on their own recommended caloric intake, which should be based on their gender, level of activity, height, and weight. This task does provide a nice connection between mathematics and health because students should have some idea of their caloric intake to maintain weight (or to gain or lose weight).

Middle school students should become aware of issues related to comparison shopping, the focus of Questions 4 and 5. Students might also investigate the costs of purchasing some of these items online and compare online prices to store prices (see for example, www.koamart.com). If desired, teachers can introduce aspects of sales tax to the cost of items.

Question 6 is meant as an extension activity. Students can compare the sizes of different versions of the snack, either in weight, dimensions, or calories. Students might be encouraged to write their investigation as a newspaper report, including information they think would be of most interest to others. Or, students could imagine writing a report about their results for a travelogue for individuals visiting a country who desire to try some of the local foods.

Hang Dry

Middle-grades students need experiences dealing with permutations and combinations. The tasks in this investigation are designed to provide such experiences. The numbers in the questions are small enough that students should be able to list the various arrangements. However, depending on the students, teachers might want to provide manipulatives that students can use to create physical examples of the different ways that the clothes can be arranged; colored cubes or pattern block pieces can easily serve to represent the different outfits.

Students should recognize that the number of different arrangements of clothes is $n!$ (Question 2c) and the probability that Sang-Woo would obtain the correct arrangment on the first try is $\frac{1}{n!}$ (Question 3). Students may be interested to learn about the factorial key on their calculator. It is an interesting exercise to ask students how large a factorial the calculator can compute before generating an error. This will vary by calculator type, but even a graphing calculator has a limit beyond which an overflow error occurs.

An extension would be to help students distinguish situations in which order matters, yielding permutations, and situations in which order does not matter, yielding combinations. For example, the order of winners in a race or the order of individuals for offices leads to permutations; the arrangement of a group of people to serve on a committee leads to combinations because only the grouping is important, not the order of the individuals within the group.

Question 4a is simply an application of multiplication. However, students may not think of this type of problem as a basic model for multiplication. Listing the possible outfits (Question 4b) provides another context for exploring probabilities. Questions 4c and 4d highlight differences between the words *and* and *or*. In Question 4c, there is only 1 outfit that satisfies the given condition, so the probability is $\frac{1}{6}$. In contrast, in Question 4d, the conditions are satisfied if the outfit has only gray pants, only a navy shirt, or both gray pants and a navy shirt; looking at the list of outfits, students can see that the probability is $\frac{4}{6}$ or $\frac{2}{3}$. Students might wonder why they cannot add the probability for gray pants and the probability for a navy shirt. The 2 conditions, gray pants and a navy shirt, are not mutually exclusive; so adding the probabilities of each separately double counts the outfit, gray pants *and* navy shirt.

Giving Directions

Being able to give and follow directions is an important life skill, including reading a coordinate grid on a map. In the movie, Sang-Woo is given very vague directions to the store that sells batteries.

Students are often not specific in the directions they provide. The tasks in this activity are designed to help them develop measurement and spatial orientation skills. Initially, students develop a set of directions for some location in the school, preferably using their classroom as the starting point; students may initially fail to indicate the starting location for the set of directions, an important point for class discussion.

Questions 2 and 3 provide an opportunity for students to use a map to provide directions from school to some local point of interest. This will likely involve the use of street names, directions for turning (either left-right or north-south-east-west) as well as some indication of distance (e.g., about 5 miles). Once students have developed their own set of directions, they should try obtaining a set of directions using any one of several Web-based sites (e.g., mapquest.com, maps.yahoo.com). When students compare their directions and the ones provided online, they should look for similarities and differences and attempt to provide some indication of why differences occurred.

Backpacking with Shoulder Poles

Students typically carry backpacks or book bags, often too heavy for their bodies. Backpacks are often better than book bags because they distribute the weight. In rural parts of Asia, shoulder poles are used to carry heavy loads and distribute the weight across the shoulders. Students are likely to think that they are carrying more than Grandma. They are likely to be quite surprised at the weight of a gallon of water and realize that Grandma is carrying about 17 pounds.

As an extension, teachers might bring in a gallon jug of water or milk (which weighs about the same as water). Students can then compare the weight of a gallon of water or milk to the weight of their books.

Reference

The Way Home. 2002. Produced by Jae-woo Hang and Woo-hyun Hang. Written and Directed by Jeong-Hyang Lee. 80 minutes. CJ Entertainment. Film.

CHAPTER 12

Children of Heaven

About the Resource

This film features an amusing story of the adventures of an adolescent, Ali, and his younger sister, Zahra, after he loses her school shoes while running errands for the family. Knowing there is no money to purchase a new pair and trying to avoid any trouble with their parents, the two secretly devise a plan to share Ali's dirty, rundown sneakers. Although they are not the best fit for Zahra's feet, she wears the shoes to her school in the mornings, and then at the same meeting place each day hurriedly hands them over to Ali so that he can wear the shoes to his school in the afternoon. As this arrangement continues, the two siblings encounter one adventure after another as they attempt to cover their tracks both at home and at school. Ali believes he has found a winning solution when he enters a districtwide children's footrace; he only needs to finish in third place to win a pair of sneakers to replace his sister's shoes.

Cultural Index			Mathematics Index	
Amenable	**Beneficial**	**Compelling**	**Explicit**	**Implicit**
	✓			✓

Cultural Group: Asian and Pacific Islanders

Length: 88 minutes

Rating: PG

Language: Farsi with English subtitles

Mathematical Focus

 Investigation: Lavash Bread

- estimating area
- area measurement
- modeling
- problem-solving strategies (determining a pattern)

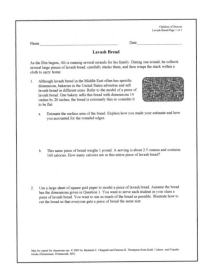

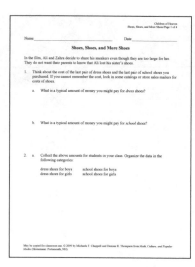

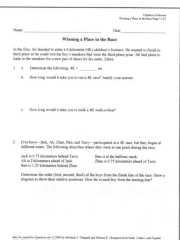

Investigation: Shoes, Shoes, and More Shoes

- collecting and organizing data
- representing data graphically
- comparing and contrasting graphical displays

Investigation: Winning a Place in the Race

- permutations
- collecting and organizing data
- problem solving

Commentary About the Investigations

These investigations can be completed independent of each other. For Shoes, Shoes, and More Shoes, teachers may want to have shoe catalogs or newspaper ads available. If students have had minimal prior experience with graphical displays, they should perhaps complete Shoes, Shoes, and More Shoes before completing Winning a Place in the Race.

Lavash Bread

Lavash bread is one type of flatbread, a kind of bread made and eaten in many cultures around the world. Before starting the activity, students might benefit from seeing some pictures of lavash bread. One source could be the Wikipedia entry on lavash bread (www.en.wikipedia.org/wiki/lavash). Also, several videos on YouTube show lavash bread and other types of Middle Eastern breads being made. You might consider having students watch some of these short videos as motivation for completing the investigation.

An initial estimate for the surface area of the bread (Question 1a) is likely to be the area of a rectangle with dimensions 14 inches by 20 inches. Students should realize that this estimate is a little high because the corners of the bread are rounded. If students outline a piece of bread with these dimensions on graph paper, they can estimate the area that is cut off each corner.

In Question 1b, students need to pay attention to units to determine the number of 2.5-ounce servings in 1 pound (16 ounces) of bread. The number of servings is not an integer and this provides an opportunity for class discussion. There are 6 full servings, leading to 960 calories. But someone could have a partial serving, accounting for the additional 64 calories. Obviously, the calories depend on a number of factors, whether low-fat or whole wheat is used, or what types of toppings might be added.

Students have an opportunity to apply problem-solving skills in Questions 2 and 3. In particular, in Question 2 they need to consider ways to divide the piece of bread into enough equal-sized pieces for everyone in class. In Question 3, students investigate a classic problem in the context of obtaining the maximum number of pieces of bread from a given number of tears. If students have access to graphing calculators, teachers might have them graph ordered pairs of the form (number of tears, maximum number of pieces) and fit a model to the data, obtaining $y = \frac{1}{2}x^2 + \frac{1}{2}x + 1$.

In the final two problems, students have an opportunity to investigate aspects of the bread of interest to them, including finding a recipe and scaling it so that enough would be made for the entire class.

Shoes, Shoes, and More Shoes

The tasks in this investigation are likely to be of particular interest to students because they are able to collect information about each other. Teachers may want to have a variety of catalogs or newspaper sales ads with shoes in case students do not recall the amount they spent for two types of shoes—dress shoes and school shoes.

In Question 2, students are expected to determine, on their own, an appropriate graphical display for the data. Students might construct bar graphs, stem-and-leaf graphs, or box-and-whisker plots. Rather than explicitly tell students what type of display to use, allow them to make their own choice and have them make at least one observation based on that choice. Then, in Question 3, students find measures of center and variability and construct a box-and-whisker plot using these values. Students who constructed a box-and-whisker plot in Question 2 should be asked to construct another type of display in Question 3. The purpose of Question 4 is to have students compare and contrast different graphical displays; students should realize that different displays provide different insights into data.

Question 6 makes connections with social studies. Many organizations collect relief supplies or clothing for individuals in need, both in the United States and in other countries. So, students can interpret their data to determine the sizes of shoes most likely to benefit adolescents in need somewhere else in the world.

Winning a Place in the Race

The tasks in this investigation are based on one of the ending scenes from the film, in which Ali tries to obtain third place in a race to win the sneakers that are the prize for this place.

For Question 1, teachers might want to have students run or walk a small portion of such a race and then extrapolate to their time for the entire 4-kilometer distance. Students might time themselves over a particular distance on the PE field, or the mathematics teacher and PE teacher might work together to coordinate the activity if they share the same students.

In Question 2, students engage in a puzzle as they use the clues to place each runner. To facilitate solving the problem, students may need to use the clues in a different order than provided. Drawing a picture is an appropriate problem-solving strategy in this situation. Students then construct their own puzzle in Question 3.

Question 5 provides another opportunity for students to organize data in an appropriate graphical display. If students have completed Shoes, Shoes, and More Shoes, then this question should be a review; otherwise, teachers may need to provide some background related to graphical displays before students proceed. If there is a 4-kilometer race run near your school's location, students should consider using data from this race as the basis for Question 5. Otherwise, an Internet search yields a variety of race sites, and students can investigate data from one race over time or multiple races, depending on their own interests.

Reference

Children of Heaven. 1999. Produced by Institute for the Intellectual Development of Children and Young Adults. Written and Directed by Majid Majidi. 88 minutes. Miramax Films. Film.

Print Literature Resources

The section contains forty-four investigations based on eighteen print resources (i.e., children's books) from four cultures: eighteen investigations from seven books featuring African or African American culture, twelve investigations from four books featuring Native American or Indigenous Peoples cultures, eight investigations from four books featuring Latino culture, and six investigations from three books featuring Asian or Pacific Islanders cultures. The investigations span the range of the five content foci recommended in the *Principles and Standards for School Mathematics* of the National Council of Teachers of Mathematics (2000).

The majority of the investigations can be completed independent of each other, so students can work on only one investigation from a particular book. Some of the investigations are easily completed in a single class period; others are more appropriate for a longer, outside-class project. The matrix, Investigations by Content and Culture, on pages xii–xiii, cross-references all the investigations by content themes; the table that follows contains only the investigations for the print literature resources. All the investigations are provided on the accompanying CD-ROM.

Reference

National Council of Teachers of Mathematics. 2000. *Principles and Standards for School Mathematics.* Reston, VA: National Council of Teachers of Mathematics.

Print Literature Investigations by Content and Culture

Resource	Number & Operations	Algebraic Thinking	Geometry	Measurement	Data Analysis & Probability
African and African American					
Beatrice's Goat	• Goat Figure • Adopt a Goat			• Goat Figure	
The Black Snowman	• Making Money Through Recycling			• Snowman: Here Today, Gone Tomorrow • Making Money Through Recycling	• Snowman: Here Today, Gone Tomorrow • Avoiding Accidents

(continues)

Resource	Number & Operations	Algebraic Thinking	Geometry	Measurement	Data Analysis & Probability
A Million Fish . . . More or Less	• Fish Loss	• Fish Loss		• Turkey Statistics • Stocking an Aquarium	• Turkey Statistics
Senefer	• Multiplication by Senefer			• Obelisks Outstanding	• Obelisks Outstanding
Village of Round and Square Houses			• House Shape	• House Shape • Cover and Recover	
Vision of Beauty	• Company Earnings • Products and Profits • It's All About "Style"				
Why Mosquitoes Buzz in People's Ears		• Actions and Consequences • Logic Rules			• The Buzz on Mosquitoes
Native American and Indigenous Peoples					
Seeing the Circle			• Constructing Circles • Will the Hidden Polygons Please Show Up?	• Sizing Up Circles	
The Cherokee	• Corn Craze	• Plentiful Harvest		• Winding Trails	
Arrow to the Sun	• Aiming to Go Far		• Is It Art? Is It Math? • Arrow Attributes • Growing in Stature	• Growing in Stature	
Buffalo Woman			• Reflections in the River • Tipi Sizes	• Tipi Sizes	
Latino					
First Day in Grapes	• Mind-Full-Paper-Less Counting • Crates of Grapes	• Crates of Grapes			
Harvesting Hope	• Walk for the Cause • Factor in the Farmers				• Factor in the Farmers
Abuela's Weave	• Fair Trade at the Marketplace		• Patterns in the Weave		
Piñatas & Smiling Skeletons	• Mexican Sweets			• Piñatas and Aguinaldos • Mexican Sweets	
Asian and Pacific Islanders					
Issunbōshi	• Living Life One Inch Tall • Timing a Journey			• Living Life One Inch Tall • Timing a Journey	
Munna and the Grain of Rice	• How a Little Becomes a Lot • Weighty Rice	• How a Little Becomes a Lot		• Weighty Rice	
The Adventures of Marco Polo	• Great Are the Numbers	• Postal Relay	• Postal Relay	• Great Are the Numbers	

CHAPTER 13

Beatrice's Goat

About the Resource

Beatrice, a nine-year-old girl in Uganda, wants to attend school but her family is unable to afford the cost of books or a uniform. When Beatrice's family receives a goat from an international project, which helps families lift themselves out of poverty, her situation starts to improve. The goat provides milk for nutrition as well as for sale.

	Cultural Index		Mathematics Index	
Amenable	**B**eneficial	**C**ompelling	Explicit	Implicit
		✓	✓	

Cultural Group: African and African American

Mathematical Focus

 Investigation: Goat Figure

- measurement (converting units)
- rational number computation (decimals and percents)

 Investigation: Adopt a Goat

- problem solving (nonroutine)

Commentary About the Investigations

Both investigations provide opportunities for students to work with number computations, including percents. Although the two investigations are independent of each other, there are some connections so that students would likely benefit from completing the two as a unit.

Goat Figure

Although cows and cow milk are more commonly available in the United States, goats, goat milk, and goat cheese are mainstays in many other parts of the world. The questions on this activity give students an opportunity to work with measurement conversions as well as with rational number computation.

The first question can have multiple solutions depending on the month that students choose to consider. In the United States, goat milk is far more expensive than cow's milk, and students could be encouraged to compare the costs for the two types of milk. Teachers might want to collect additional information about goat milk before using this lesson. Two useful sites are www.dairyfoodsconsulting.com and www.whfoods.com.

The data on the daily calorie intake in Question 2b are for males and females at the full height and weight range (see recommendations at www.medindia.net and www.uabhealth.org). The parts of Question 2 are linked, and students will need to use their answers in one part to obtain an answer for other parts. For instance, for males, 1 cup of goat milk provides about 6.7% of the daily intake ($168 \div 2{,}500$), of which 500 to 750 calories should come from fat. If 9 calories equal 1 gram of fat, then 500 to 750 calories is 56 to 83 grams of fat. Likewise, 1 cup (8 ounces) of goat milk is 10 grams of fat, or 12–18% of the daily recommended requirement. In many parts of the world, access to goat milk on a regular basis can help provide necessary nutrition for children. Depending on school policies relative to food, teachers might want to bring some goat milk or goat cheese to class and let students taste a sample.

Adopt a Goat

This investigation encourages students to think about how they might be able to help others around the world. There are several organizations that provide aid to families by giving them resources that are self-sustaining. We reference two in the investigation. Question 3 engages students in nonroutine problem solving that could lead to fundraising for an organization that helps those less fortunate.

As an extension, interested students could investigate Web resources about starting a small garden in their backyard. They could research questions like: What produce could they grow? How much could they grow? How much of their own vegetables could they provide to others? Many people grow tomatoes or herbs in window pots or on backyard patios. Students could be encouraged to investigate the costs involved in such activities and the amount of money that might be saved by growing some of one's own food.

Reference

McBrier, Page. 2001. *Beatrice's Goat.* New York: Atheneum.

CHAPTER 14

Senefer: A Young Genius in Old Egypt

About the Resource

The story of *Senefer* is inspired by the life of Ah'mose, a famous Egyptian scribe credited with compiling the Rhind Mathematical Papyrus from which much of the knowledge of Egyptian mathematics is derived. Senefer's adventures and mathematical prowess eventually led to his admission into the school for scribes where he learned to compute with numbers. He also planned to become an engineer so that he could build and raise great obelisks to record Egypt's accomplishments.

Cultural Index			Mathematics Index	
Amenable	**B**eneficial	**C**ompelling	**E**xplicit	**I**mplicit
		✓	✓	

Cultural Group: African and African American

Mathematical Focus

 Investigation: Multiplication by Senefer

- number operations
- patterns in operations
- problem solving

 Investigation: Obelisks Outstanding

- measurement
- data analysis
- ratio and proportional reasoning

Commentary About the Investigations

These two investigations can be completed independent of each other. For Obelisks Outstanding, students should have access to the Internet to explore some history related to famous obelisks; this investigation has interesting social studies connections.

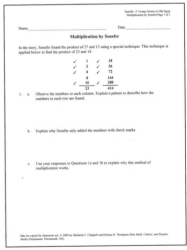

Multiplication by Senefer

This investigation introduces students to an alternative approach for multiplication they may never have seen. This method of Egyptian doubling can be applied to a wide range of problems. For students who may still struggle with the typical multiplication algorithm, Egyptian doubling may prove beneficial because students only need to double and add. Students can double simply by adding a number to itself.

In Questions 1 and 2, students explore using the method with natural numbers; they should understand that the method works because the underlying mathematics relates to the distributive property. Question 3 is designed to help students recognize the applicability of this method to computations with fractions and decimals, operations that often pose difficulties for many middle-grades students.

Obelisks Outstanding

In this investigation, students explore data about ancient obelisks using resources on the Web. They are encouraged to find structures in their community or state that are obelisk-shaped. Many students might mention the Washington Monument as an example of an obelisk-shaped structure with which they are familiar (Question 2).

The PBS website lists information, including pictures, of twelve of the twenty-one ancient Egyptian obelisks still in existence. Students can easily explore this website to learn information about each of the obelisks (Question 3). Because the Pharaoh under which the obelisk was constructed is also listed, this investigation has some nice connections to social studies.

The sizes of these obelisks are quite massive. So, to put these structures in perspective, students can consider how many middle-grades students it would take to match the height or weight of their favorite obelisk (Question 4). Although this number will vary based on the representative height or weight of a student and the height or weight of the selected obelisk, the height is likely to be equivalent to 12 to 18 students and the weight to more than 2,400 students.

Question 5, focusing on scale models, gives students an opportunity to consider ratios and proportional reasoning. Last, students are to name general items that might have the shape of an obelisk (Question 6), gather further research on these interesting structures, including numerical information, and summarize in a brief report (Question 7).

Reference

Lumpkin, Beatrice. 1991. *Senefer: A Young Genius in Old Egypt.* Trenton, NJ: African World Press.

CHAPTER 15

The Village of Round and Square Houses

About the Resource

This story, told from the perspective of a native from the African village of Tos in Cameroon, explains the origin of an unusual village tradition. When the local volcano on Naka Mountain erupted, only

Cultural Index			Mathematics Index	
Amenable	**B**eneficial	**C**ompelling	**E**xplicit	**I**mplicit
		✓	✓	

two houses survived—one round and one square. As the villagers worked together to rebuild their village after the eruption, the women lived in the round house and the men in the square house. After the work was finished, the villagers continued to live in different-shaped houses based on gender.

Cultural Group: African and African American

Mathematical Focus

 Investigation: House Shape

- exploring geometrical shapes
- measurement, particularly circumference and area of circles

 Investigation: Cover and Recover

- measurement, particularly finding area

Commentary About the Investigations

Although the two investigations in this chapter can be completed independent of each other, Cover and Recover may be more meaningful for students if they have first completed House Shape, in which they explore features of round houses. Access to the Internet is recommended for both investigations so that students can locate floor plans of houses.

House Shape

The investigation engages students in exploring the shapes of different houses, including those that are polygonal (e.g., square) and those considered circular in nature (e.g., octagonal). Students should realize that the shape of the floor plan, which provides a footprint for a house, is used as the basis for determining its shape.

Initially, students may brainstorm different house shapes they have observed in their own communities or cities (Question 1). This will connect the investigation to the story and enable students to think about possible similarities and differences between the square and round houses in the village of Tos. The Internet can be a useful tool in such explorations and brainstorming because many homes are now pictured on the Internet, either as part of real-estate pages or as unusual dwellings (Question 2).

For Question 3, we found floor plans of round houses on the Internet with a simple Google search for *round houses* (e.g., www.deltechomes.com or www.hgtv.com). Many houses labeled as round are technically polygonal, but with a large number of sides (such as 18). Nevertheless, the shape is close to being round, so formulas for the circumference and area of circles can be used to estimate the perimeter and living area of these polygonal homes. If floor plans with dimensions cannot be located, students can download an outline of a floor plan, measure the dimensions of the floor plan with a ruler, and then determine an appropriate scale between the floor plan and the actual home before trying to find the perimeter and living area of the home.

At the time of writing this chapter, the round earthen homes in Fujian Province in China had been designated as a UNESCO World Heritage Site, and a relatively short video documentary about these homes was available on the Web (shanghaiist.com/2008/08/07/video_the_earthen_roundhouses_of_fu.php). Teachers may want to download the video and show it as part of a class discussion about round houses. Such a video also integrates social studies and geography into the mathematics classroom.

In Questions 5 and 6, students explore different-shaped houses from a variety of cultures around the world. Teachers might choose to assign each group a different-shaped house and then have groups make short presentations to the rest of the class. This approach gives students an opportunity to learn about house shapes of many different cultures while only exploring one shape themselves.

Cover and Recover

In this investigation, students have the opportunity to compare floor plans and determine the cost of covering the floor with three different types of materials. To begin, students may explore the Internet to see and download different floor plans of houses, which can be used to address the questions within the investigation, starting with the floor area of the house (Question 1).

For Question 2, teachers might bring in catalogs or newspaper advertisements with various costs of carpet, tile, and hardwood. Different groups could explore costs of different qualities of materials for the same floor plans. As an alternative, teachers could have students work in groups, with each group determining the costs for a single type of material and then sharing results with other groups addressing costs of different materials. This problem helps students recognize that people often have to make decisions when furnishing or remodeling a house and that costs are part of the decision-making process.

For the final question, students might make scale models of furniture and consider placing that furniture in a room of the house. Students may not realize that people often use this strategy when rearranging furniture to avoid moving heavy furniture pieces multiple times.

Reference

Grifalconi, Ann. 1986. *The Village of Round and Square Houses*. Boston: Little, Brown and Company.

CHAPTER 16

Why Mosquitoes Buzz in People's Ears

About the Resource

Cultural Index			Mathematics Index	
Amenable	**B**eneficial	**C**ompelling	**E**xplicit	**I**mplicit
		✓		✓

A Winner of the Caldecott Award, *Why Mosquitoes Buzz in People's Ears* is an African tale about the dangers of leaping to conclusions without any evidence. A string of events in the animal kingdom causes the death of an owlet; as a consequence, the owl fails to hoot to wake the sun. So, the lion convenes a meeting with all the animals involved, except the mosquito, who is the actual instigator of the events. Once the mosquito learns that the other animals want to punish her, she becomes afraid and spends the rest of her life inquiring (buzzing) in people's ears to determine if the animals are still angry.

Cultural Group: African and African American

Mathematical Focus

 Investigation: Actions and Consequences

- identifying sequence of actions
- developing flowcharts for a sequence of actions

 Investigation: Logic Rules

- symbolizing conditionals
- drawing conclusions in arguments using conditionals

Investigation: The Buzz on Mosquitoes

- synthesizing facts
- problem solving

Commentary About the Investigations

Mathematical reasoning is important in proofs as well as in everyday reasoning but is often reserved for students in advanced grades. However, this resource presents a delightful story that introduces students to basic concepts related to mathematical logic and reasoning. Actions and Consequences and Logic Rules should be completed together because Actions and Consequences provides the background needed for Logic Rules.

Actions and Consequences

In this investigation, students identify each event that occurs in the story and focus on how one event sparks another. The chain of events offers a great example of mathematical reasoning, setting the stage for conditional *if–then* statements to be introduced in Logic Rules. Logic and mathematical reasoning are not heavily emphasized in middle schools, yet students need work with reasoning as preparation for advanced mathematics as well as life.

In Question 1, students identify the major events based on the behavior of each animal (e.g., the mosquito annoys the iguana). Then in Question 2, students link the events, showing how one event generated another. They draw a simple flowchart diagram linking two events. Although students may skip events included in the story, they should be able to connect an *action* to a resulting *consequence*. Students compare flowcharts with peers in Question 3.

Logic Rules

In this investigation, students symbolize the various actions in the story and then write implications (i.e., conditionals) using those implications. In Questions 1 and 2, students simply symbolize the events of the story.

In Question 3, students link the implications together to create simple arguments. Throughout, students are using the form of a hypothetical syllogism, namely

A implies *B*.
B implies *C*.
Therefore, *A* implies *C*.

Teachers might help students connect an argument based on a hypothetical syllogism to their number work with the transitive property (i.e., if $a = b$ and $b = c$, then $a = c$). In Question 3c, students should realize that no conclusion can be drawn because there is no way to link the two implications together. In contrast, a conclusion can be drawn from the implications in Question 3d; however, students must rearrange the implications in order to link them together.

Question 4 could be a good challenge for students to rewrite the story in terms of implications. Students might work in small groups to record the entire story on chart paper and then compare their work with that of other groups.

The Buzz on Mosquitoes

This investigation provides an opportunity for students to investigate facts about mosquitoes. There are numerous Internet sites that students could use. We found the fact in Question 1 using the website www.howstuffworks.com/mosquito.htm, which also includes pictures of mosquitoes and a video about mosquito control.

Reference

Aardema, Verna. 1975. *Why Mosquitoes Buzz in People's Ears.* New York: Puffin Pied Paper Books.

CHAPTER 17

The Black Snowman

About the Resource

Jacob is tired of being poor and black. As Christmas approaches, his family has no money to buy presents from other than the hand-me-down store. One day, Jacob and his brother build a snowman from

Cultural Index			Mathematics Index	
Amenable	**B**eneficial	**C**ompelling	Explicit	Implicit
		✓		✓

dirty snow and cover it with a piece of cloth found in the trash. The cloth is not any piece of cloth but a piece of African kente cloth; the cloth bestows its magic upon the snowman and gives him the power to speak. The snowman helps Jacob realize he is descended from African warriors and has a heritage of which to be proud. When Jacob's younger brother becomes trapped in a building on fire, the snowman helps Jacob find the courage to rescue his brother.

Cultural Group: African and African American

Mathematical Focus

 Investigation: Snowman: Here Today, Gone Tomorrow

- determining volume for spheres and rectangular prisms
- determining surface area for spheres and rectangular prisms

 Investigation: Avoiding Accidents

- displaying data
- describing trends in data

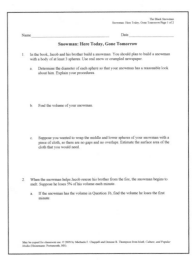

Investigation: Making Money Through Recycling

- computations with rational numbers
- determining volume of a cylinder

Commentary About the Investigations

Each investigation is independent of the others and directly relates to the context of the story. Collectively, they provide opportunities for students to engage in finding volume, surface area, and rates; display data; and compute with rational numbers.

Snowman: Here Today, Gone Tomorrow

This investigation provides an opportunity for students to use the formulas $V = \frac{4}{3}\pi r^3$ and $SA = 4\pi r^2$ to find the volume and surface area of a sphere, respectively. Depending on their location, students may never have had an opportunity to make an actual snowman. However, students can use crumpled newspaper in place of snow. Because students can design their snowmen with different overall sizes and with different ratios among the diameters of the 3 spheres comprising the snowman, students should expect to justify their solutions. As in the story, a kente cloth would not cover the top sphere, which represents the head. Students should realize that covering the middle and lower spheres with a cloth corresponds to finding the surface area of these spheres.

Many students may evaluate Question 2 by finding 5%, subtracting from the original volume, and then repeating the process over and over. With a calculator, this is feasible, even if not efficient. To foster algebraic thinking, students might be encouraged to look for patterns. If the snowman loses 5% of his volume each minute, he keeps 95% of the volume. So, each minute he has 95% of the volume from the previous minute. Thus, the volume after n minutes is given by $V = 0.95^n \times$ original volume.

Question 3 provides an opportunity to give the mathematics classroom the feel of a science laboratory. Students collect data from an experiment and then determine an appropriate display. In this case, students should graph the data on a coordinate grid, placing the number of minutes along the horizontal axis and the volume along the vertical axis; such a graph displays the trends in the data over time.

Avoiding Accidents

Becoming aware of safety is important for young adolescents. Teachers will need to use knowledge of their students to determine whether the given activity is appropriate or likely to be too sensitive for use with students. For instance, if there has recently been a death among students at the school, the activity might be too emotional for use.

Fires are a serious cause of injury or death, and home fires are typically devastating to families, who often lose everything. Students can look at data to determine which months are the most deadly. If teachers don't want to have students look at data for their own town, they might have students look at data for college campuses, available at www.campus-firewatch.com.

After looking at the data, students might be encouraged to research whether they have working smoke detectors at home, how many, and in what rooms of the house. That data could then be collated for students and some safety tips could be provided, thus blending mathematics with health. In areas where fuel oil furnaces or wood-burning stoves are used, students might also collect data about carbon monoxide detectors; every year, people die from carbon monoxide poisoning, which could be prevented with some type of alarm.

Making Money Through Recycling

Recycling is big business. In many states, consumers pay a deposit for cans or bottles, yet they toss the cans or bottles in the trash rather than return them to the store for a deposit. The questions in this activity help students realize how much money might be saved or earned through recycling. Many interesting facts about aluminum and recycling can be found on the Internet.

In Question 1b, about 1,000 cans or bottles are needed to earn $50 at 5 cents per can. For a class of 30 students, this amounts to a little more than 30 cans or bottles per student (Question 1c). Over the course of the year, this seems to be a reasonable number. In the remainder of the questions, students think about the space occupied by a can and how much space might be saved if the can were crushed. As an extension, teachers might consider having students try to crush empty cans by hand and then compare the heights of the crushed cans to the height of an uncrushed can. If a compacter is accessible, students might compare heights of manually crushed cans to those crushed by a machine.

For the last question, students should be encouraged to work in groups to develop a recycling plan. Groups could be encouraged to share their results with the entire class for comment. Perhaps the plans could be merged to develop a recycling plan for the entire school. If the community has a recycling plan, students could investigate the amount of different materials recycled in the community each year as well as the amount of money the community earns from recycling.

Reference

Mendez, Phil. 1989. *The Black Snowman*. New York: Scholastic.

CHAPTER 18

A Million Fish . . . More or Less

About the Resource

Cultural Index			Mathematics Index	
Amenable	**B**eneficial	**C**ompelling	**E**xplicit	**I**mplicit
✓				✓

In this story, a young boy goes to the Louisiana bayou and catches a million fish. However, on his way home, he encounters a number of obstacles involving other animals whose habitat is in the bayou, and thus, he loses all but three fish. His story is one more tale added to the other strange tales of the bayou.

Cultural Group: African and African American

Mathematical Focus

Investigation: Turkey Statistics

- numerical computations
- measurement
- data analysis

Investigation: Fish Loss

- number sense
- algebraic reasoning

 Investigation: Stocking an Aquarium

* measurement (weight)

Commentary About the Investigations

The three investigations in this chapter are independent of each other. For Stocking an Aquarium, teachers might want to have available in class an empty aquarium.

Turkey Statistics

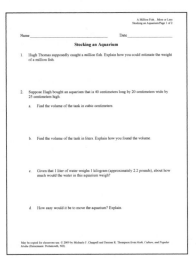

This investigation uses facts about turkeys to engage students in numerical computation, measurement, and data analysis. In addition, students have an opportunity to use Internet resources to locate information needed to answer problems.

In Questions 1 and 2, students have an opportunity to think about quantities that might weigh 500 pounds. Large turkeys typically weigh about 35 pounds. Many students are challenged when asked to make estimates about measurement. One way to think about this quantity is to consider it as the weight of about 4 or 5 middle school students.

Questions 3 and 4 require students to collect information about their class and use the data to solve problems. Specifically, in Question 4 students must represent the data in some graphical way. Bar graphs and pictographs are appropriate ways to display the data, as are circle graphs. Given that the data represent the entire class and there is no overlap because students provided their *favorite* meat, the data can be represented as a circle graph; with this graphical display, students have an opportunity to use percents and angle measures to construct an accurate graph.

Questions 7–9 are open-ended and students generate their own choices to complete the problems. In Question 7, cultural factors come into play as students decide what other foods will accompany the turkey. Students can be encouraged to compare their choices and the amount the cafeteria needs for the student body to the national consumption of foods eaten at Thanksgiving, such as cranberry sauce, sweet potatoes, or pumpkin. There are many possibilities for facts to complete Question 9, such as the cooking time per pound, the cost of import sales of live turkeys from Canada, or the nutritional value of turkey.

Several Internet sites may be of use to students in completing this investigation, including the following:

www.factmonster.com/spot/tgturkeyfacts.html
www.teachervision.com/lesson-plans/lesson-2418.html
www.urbanext.uiuc.edu/turkey/facts.html

Fish Loss

In this investigation, students use number sense and algebraic reasoning as they draw on the information in the story plot and examine the feasibility of the story's numbers. In Question 1, students should record as much information as possible in the given chart, which serves as an organizing tool for the information. Initially, an exponential decay pattern of fish loss is suggested; however, the pattern seems not to hold due to the lack of specific amounts provided for each scenario. However, students can still explore the notion of limits in that the number of fish reduces substantially each time and, at the end of the story, represents a small fraction of the amount initially stated. Also, students can use variables and expressions to represent the unknown quantities.

Question 2 reverses the story plot; in this case, students explore an exponential growth pattern with more specificity. Students use multiple representations in the form of a table and a graph. If students create their graphs by hand, comparisons can later be made to graphs created using graphing technology. This investigation ends with students writing observations about their graphs (Question 2d).

Stocking an Aquarium

Students focus on measurement in this investigation; they consider how estimates of the weight of a large quantity of fish might be made. Many different suggestions are likely to arise. A class discussion provides an avenue for talking about the advantages and disadvantages of different methods.

In Question 2, students use actual dimensions of an aquarium to determine volume and the weight of an aquarium filled with water. Students need to use the fact that 1000 cubic centimeters of water is equivalent to 1 liter of water, which weighs 1 kilogram (or about 2.2 pounds). So, the given aquarium would weigh about 35 pounds.

In Question 3, students have an opportunity to compare three different recommendations for the number of inches of fish that can be stocked in an aquarium. The recommendation in Question 3b provides a maximum for the number of inches. Students might need help realizing that the question asks for the *number of inches* of fish and not the actual number of fish.

Finally, in Question 4, students consider how many aquariums would be needed for a million fish. Notice here that students first need to consider how many inches they would have with a million fish because all three recommendations for stocking an aquarium (in Question 3) relate to inches. Students should be encouraged to estimate the length of a fish they would keep and use this estimate to determine the number of inches for a million fish.

As an extension, if students live near a large aquarium that serves as a tourist attraction, then teachers can have students research facts about the number of fish held at the aquarium. In addition, www.thetropicaltank.co.uk/tanks-us.htm is an Internet site with useful information about stocking aquariums.

Reference

McKissack, Patricia C. 1992. *A Million Fish . . . More or Less.* New York: Alfred A. Knopf.

CHAPTER **19**

Vision of Beauty: The Story of Sarah Breedlove Walker

About the Resource

Cultural Index			Mathematics Index	
Amenable	**B**eneficial	**C**ompelling	**E**xplicit	**I**mplicit
		✓	✓	

Written as a biography, this story describes the life of Sarah Breedlove Walker (alias, Madam C. J. Walker), who lived from the mid-1800s to the early 1900s. Though born in poverty in Louisiana, near the Mississippi Delta, she was a business pioneer, creating hair and beauty care products for black women. Madam Walker ultimately established her own manufacturing company, which became one of the largest companies in America at the time and a great financial success, surviving for more than seventy-eight years. Although Madam Walker died at the age of fifty-one, her legacy of wealth and philanthropy in the African American community continues until this day.

Cultural Group: African and African American

Mathematical Focus

Investigation: Company Earnings

- numerical computations
- computations with percents, including percent increase
- compound interest

Investigation: Products and Profits

- problem solving
- percents, including finding commission

70

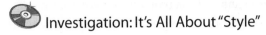

Investigation: It's All About "Style"

- problem solving
- computations, including with percent

Commentary About the Investigations

The three investigations can be assigned independent of each other. For Company Earnings, students will need to take information directly from the book.

Company Earnings

This investigation incorporates information from the book about the successful beginning years of Mme. Walker's manufacturing company. Specifically, the book provides the weekly earnings for a Walker agent at the time and compares these earnings to typical earnings for a black woman, a black man, and a white man. Students will need to complete the table (Question 1a) before they determine the minimal number of Walker agents that were employed by the company during 1908 and 1911 (Questions 1b and 1c). Students then use their responses to determine the percent of employee growth (Question 1d), which deals with the concept of *percent increase*. Students may want to find what percent of 80 is 600, rather than find what percent the increase is of 80. For either case, it is likely that students will need to discuss how to convert 6.5 to an appropriate percent.

Question 2 focuses on the amount of earnings that the company generated annually. Students need to compare these earnings with current earnings from a modest 3 percent inflation rate (Question 2b), introducing students to the concept of compound interest. Through this computation, students should realize why the earnings of Mme. Walker's company were so impressive for the early 1900s.

The revenue growth of the company from Question 2c and the employee growth rate from Question 1d are the same; this might not always be the case. However, in these simplified problems, all employees receive the same salary so that increases in earnings are directly related to increases in personnel. Students should discuss this percentage growth (650%), which signifies phenomenal growth for a company over a three-year period (1908–1911). Students might research business websites to compare Mme. Walker's business growth to that for a typical current-day small business.

Products and Profits

This investigation simulates the situation described in the book in which Mme. C. J. Walker began her company by demonstrating hair care products to women in their own homes. Today, many hair care distributors work in a similar manner, delivering professional hair care products directly to stylists in their own salons. A number of the products listed in the table are common across racial and ethnic groups. However, because

Madam Walker was a black entrepreneur and sold hair products for black women, some products in the table might be more recognizable among black females than among individuals from other groups. Teachers might begin this investigation by surveying their students about the common hair care products they use and the general costs for these products. Teachers could then build an extension to the investigation using these items and costs.

For this investigation, students determine the monthly, quarterly, and annual incomes for the distributor, Dorothy, given the base salary and the rate of commission (Questions 1, 2, and 3). Because of the computations needed, teachers might have students work in groups, with each group computing the sales and commission for a given month or for a quarter. Groups can then pool their results together. Teachers may want to have students compute the total amount of sales per month and check those values before having students determine the monthly commissions (Question 3). In Question 4, students simply interpret their results for the various months.

Students will need to use problem-solving skills in Questions 5 and 6. If students know the basic salary ($2,200), then they can determine the total amount paid in commissions and work backward to determine the amount of sales. Many combinations of product numbers are possible at the monthly level to generate the total required in sales.

If students have access to spreadsheets, they could complete the entire investigation using this tool. With a spreadsheet, students can create a formula for total sales; they can observe how the total changes as the number of products sold changes.

It's All About "Style"

This investigation helps students think more about annual costs they (or their parents/guardians) may spend on their own hair care. Although we have provided costs for common salon services, such prices tend to vary greatly across cities and regions, so teachers should feel free to change the given prices in order to reflect local salon costs. Teachers should be aware that amounts spent on hair may fluctuate greatly across students from different racial and ethnic backgrounds. Depending on the demographics at the school and potential socioeconomic levels, teachers may need to use this investigation with care.

There are multiple solutions possible to this investigation, depending on individual style and preferences. Students should be required to demonstrate that their budget plans meet all the given criteria.

Reference

Lasky, Kathryn. 2000. *Vision of Beauty: The Story of Sarah Breedlove Walker.* Cambridge: Candlewick.

Seeing the Circle

About the Resource

As a featured title in a Meet the Author series, this book presents a brief look into the life of author Joseph Bruchac, who details his typical daily routine as he develops and writes his books. Bruchac, a

Cultural Index			Mathematics Index	
Amenable	**B**eneficial	**C**ompelling	**Explicit**	**Implicit**
		✓	✓	

Native American author of over sixty books, shares how he became a storyteller and writer. Through personal photos, he describes a circle design given to him by a Mohegan elder who also explained the meaning behind the four parts into which the circle is divided. The book is encouraging to those interested in becoming a professional writer or storyteller.

Cultural Group: Native American and Indigenous Peoples

Mathematical Focus

 ### Investigation: Constructing Circles

- parts of a circle
- geometric construction with drawing tools

 ### Investigation: Will the Hidden Polygons Please Show Up?

- geometric figures, including properties of figures
- spatial visualization

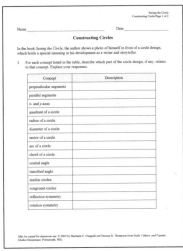

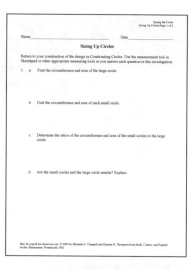

 Investigation: Sizing Up Circles

- measurement of circles, including circumference and area
- distance and midpoint formulas

Commentary About the Investigations

All of the investigations surround the circle design as illustrated in the book. Students should complete Constructing Circles before they work on the remaining investigations. If students do not have access to Geometer's Sketchpad, they can use a simple compass and straightedge construction tools. More than likely, doing all three investigations will require more than one class period.

Constructing Circles

Students first observe the circle design in the book to think about the geometrical relationships inherent in it (Question 1). There are many geometric concepts embedded in the circle design, and teachers should provide ample time for students to think about these concepts. Some students may not have encountered certain terms or ideas, but a teacher may use the design as an illustrative example of the concept. Teachers might consider having students work together in small groups to complete the table.

There are several ways to construct the circle design (Question 2), whether using a compass and straightedge or Geometer's Sketchpad. A low-cost alternative might be to use small, circular paper plates. Students can fold the plates two ways to determine the center of the circle and then construct the smaller circles in each of the four quadrants. Students could label concepts from the table in Question 1 on various circle designs.

Will the Hidden Polygons Please Show Up?

This investigation requires students to revisit various polygons as they could appear in the circle design. It is highly probable that students will have heard of many of these polygons from earlier grades; in fact, many of these polygons have been studied to some extent in the elementary grades. But students often forget the properties of the shapes or have not investigated them. In particular, students may not have seen the term *regular* as applied to polygons and may need to discuss that regular polygons have all sides congruent and all angles congruent.

The constructions require students to think about the shape's properties in order to construct it according to the given specification. Students should be expected to determine length measurements or angle measurements to verify that the constructed polygon is indeed the figure requested (i.e., to verify that a figure is a square, students should verify that the sides are all congruent and the angle measures are all 90°).

Sizing Up Circles

Students may or may not have had prior experience working with the circumference and area formulas of circles. If students are using Sketchpad, they do not need to use a formula for the investigation; they can simply use the Measurement tool on Sketchpad as a "black box." However, if students do not have access to Sketchpad, then teachers may need to engage students with some prerequisite activities related to the circumference and area of a circle prior to completing Sizing Up Circles.

Depending on the grade level and course experiences of students, they may not have previously used the distance or midpoint formulas (Question 3). The distance formula is a good application of the Pythagorean Theorem, and teachers might use the theorem to help students understand how it is derived. The midpoint formula is simply an application of averages. Both formulas provide an opportunity for students to identify coordinates on a grid and then substitute those coordinates into a formula. So these questions help provide exploration into algebraic concepts.

Reference

Bruchac, Joseph. 1999. *Seeing the Circle.* Katonah, NY: Richard C. Owen.

CHAPTER 21

The Cherokee

About the Resource

This book is one of several in the Watts Library collection of books written about Native American tribes. Formatted in small chapters, the book describes the beliefs, traditions, and practices of the Cherokee, including a historical account of their forced relocation in 1838–1839 from their original homelands in eight southeastern states (Alabama, Georgia, Kentucky, North Carolina, South Carolina, Tennessee, Virginia, West Virginia) to Indian Territory in what is now Oklahoma. Those who moved to the Indian Territory are known today as the Western Cherokee; those who remained in the southeast are called the Eastern Cherokee. The book concludes with a glimpse into modern Cherokee life as well as a time line of major events for the Cherokee people.

Cultural Index			Mathematics Index	
Amenable	**B**eneficial	**C**ompelling	**E**xplicit	**I**mplicit
		✓		✓

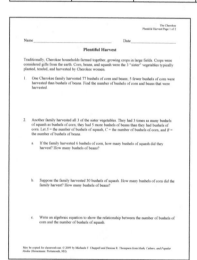

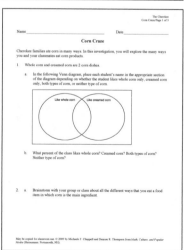

Cultural Group: Native American and Indigenous Peoples

Mathematical Focus

 Investigation: Plentiful Harvest

- writing algebraic equations
- solving systems of linear equations

 Investigation: Corn Craze

- interpreting Venn diagrams, including intersections and unions
- problem solving

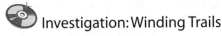

Investigation: Winding Trails

- reading and interpreting maps
- using ratios, particularly scales on a map

Commentary About the Investigations

These investigations build on ideas from two of the book's six chapters, respectively titled "Origins" and "Trail of Tears." Each investigation is independent of the other.

Plentiful Harvest

The tasks in this investigation give students an opportunity to write algebraic equations meeting specific conditions and then solve systems of linear equations. Question 1 provides a gentle introduction to systems of linear equations. Students can also solve this problem using guess-and-check. However, they should realize that their solution must satisfy two conditions: the total number of bushels of beans and corn must equal 77 *and* the number of bushels of corn must be 5 fewer than the number of bushels of beans. Teachers should discuss different ways that the solution can be found, such as by writing equations, building tables, guessing and checking, or drawing diagrams.

Question 2 begins by having students explore the task with specific numbers before they write algebraic expressions. Many students grapple at writing an appropriate equation for a relationship such as "3 times as many bushels of squash (S) as bushels of corn (C)," often writing the relationship incorrectly as $3S = C$ rather than correctly as $S = 3C$. Completing a couple of items with numerical relationships first should help students write the algebraic relationship appropriately. Although this question involves a system of three linear equations in three unknowns, the system is easily solved by substituting for the variables.

Question 3 provides another opportunity for students to solve a system of linear equations in three unknowns. Unlike Question 2 in which students are guided toward a setup and solution, in Question 3 students must complete the entire setup and solution on their own. Although completing this investigation is beneficial regardless of the course students are enrolled in, it is particularly important for students who are not enrolled in a formal algebra course.

Corn Craze

In this investigation, students have an opportunity to work with Venn diagrams, including intersections and unions. The first question is designed to help students think about where elements would be placed in the diagram. Students place their name based on their likes or dislikes of the two types of corn; most students have an intuitive understanding about where names should be placed when students like both types of corn. Students should realize that the entire rectangle represents the universal set of all students.

In Question 1b, students determine the percent of the universal set in each region. Students need to recognize that the number of students who like whole corn consists of two regions—the region representing students who like *only* whole corn and the students who like *both* whole corn and creamed corn. That is, the number of students who like whole corn is the sum of the numbers in the two regions inside the whole corn circle. Likewise, the number of students who like creamed corn is the sum of the numbers in the two regions inside the creamed corn circle. Students should realize that the total number of students who like at least one type of corn is *not* the sum of the number who like whole corn and the number who like creamed corn, because those who like both (in the intersection) would be counted twice. A discussion of this issue can help prepare students for the problem-solving task in Question 3.

Question 2 enables students to build a Venn diagram based on their likes and dislikes related to corn foods. There are many possibilities that students might list, including the following:

corn pudding	corn nuts
fried corn	cornmeal
corn flakes	corn bread
corn soup	corn on the cob
grilled corn	corn stew
corn chips	corn casserole
creamed corn	whole corn
yellow corn	white corn

After students group their suggestions into three categories and label each with a meaningful label, they should once again place their names in the appropriate sections of the three-circle Venn diagram.

Question 3 is a problem-solving task involving Venn diagrams. It is not uncommon for students to place 26 (for the number of students who like corn bread) in the portion of the circle that represents those who *only* like corn bread; students may need assistance recognizing that this number represents the sum of all the sections of the corn bread circle. This is a good task for cooperative group work so that students can talk about how the numbers need to be placed within the Venn diagram.

As an extension, teachers might have students research recipes related to favorite corn products. Students could then determine how much of each ingredient would be needed in order to prepare enough of the recipe for the entire class.

Winding Trails

In this investigation, students have an opportunity to read and interpret maps, including using map scales to estimate distances. The distances obtained in Question 3 are likely to be rough estimates, depending on how students measure along the winding trails. For Question 4, teachers should obtain a current U.S. map or state maps for those states included along the Trail of Tears. Some maps have mileage charts to indicate distances between pairs of cities. Students can also total distances along roads by reading the distance markers on the map between two locations. Many students may never have read a map at such a level of detail, so teachers may need to spend some time getting students started. An interesting exercise is to compare the distance obtained from the mileage chart or from adding up the distances along the pathway with the distance obtained by measuring the length between two cities and using the map scale.

In Question 5, students compare the time for this journey by walking and traveling by car. Given that a car travels at about 60 miles per hour and a person walks at about 2–3 miles per hour, it is likely surprising for students to observe that the walking time is about 20–30 times the number of hours traveled by car. Students should be encouraged to translate the time in hours to a number of days in order to comprehend the time.

Teachers might also explore websites for current and historical maps. A Google search yields numerous possible websites related to the Trail of Tears.

Reference

Sonneborn, Liz. 2003. *The Cherokee*. New York: Franklin Watts of Scholastic.

CHAPTER 22

Arrow to the Sun:
A Pueblo Indian Tale

About the Resource

Cultural Index			Mathematics Index	
Amenable	**B**eneficial	**C**ompelling	Explicit	Implicit
		✓		✓

In this Pueblo Indian tale, a young boy goes in search of his father. As he seeks help from individuals in the community, he encounters Arrow Maker, who realizes the young boy has been sent from the Sun. So, Arrow Maker remakes the boy into a special arrow and then shoots the arrow toward the Sun. When the boy meets the Sun, he has to endure four ceremonies to determine whether the Sun is really his father. After the boy passes each test, he is sent back to the Earth and his return is celebrated in the Dance of Life.

Cultural Group: Native American and Indigenous Peoples

Mathematical Focus

 Investigation: Is It Art? Is It Math?

- reflection and rotation symmetry
- recognizing geometric shapes
- identifying geometric concepts in figures

Investigation: Arrow Attributes

- spatial sense, including drawing diagrams
- geometric shapes and notations, including labeling diagrams according to specific conditions
- congruency of segments and triangles
- reasoning with justifications

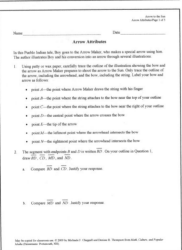

Investigation: Growing in Stature

- size and scale changes
- similar figures

 Investigation: Aiming to Go Far

- number sense, particularly with large numbers
- problem solving

Commentary About the Investigations

Investigations can be completed independently. However, it may be helpful for students to complete Is It Art? Is It Math? before working on other investigations as students will focus on the illustrations in this story. Both Arrow Attributes and Growing in Stature are also based on the beautiful story illustrations. For Arrow Attributes, students will need some type of patty paper or wax paper as well as some tracing markers so they can prove relationships informally. For Growing in Stature, students will need color tiles or pattern blocks; if these are not available, teachers may have students use virtual manipulatives to draw their figure person on the computer (see nlvm.usu.edu/).

Is It Art? Is It Math?

Although investigations can be completed independent of each other, this first investigation calls attention to the art in the book, which provides the basis for the tasks in several other investigations. It is important that students carefully justify their responses in each case. For instance, some of the Pot Maker's clay pots exhibit reflection symmetry but others do not. If students have traced the illustration onto another piece of paper, they should be expected to draw the line of symmetry for those pots with reflection symmetry or place a straw or piece of spaghetti on the line in the actual book.

Arrow Attributes

In this investigation, students study the characteristics of the bow and arrow in the illustration in the story. Many geometric properties are embedded in the illustration, and the series of tasks in this investigation helps students recognize these properties. In Question 1, students have an opportunity to label a diagram based on a series of descriptions and conditions. This is an important skill that helps students develop their spatial sense and geometric thinking. As students draw the figure, they should simply outline the bow and arrow and not focus on drawing all the intricate details of the illustration. Students might use rulers, but only as a straightedge tool to be accurate in drawing straight lines. In Questions 2, 4, 5, and 6, students should be able to use

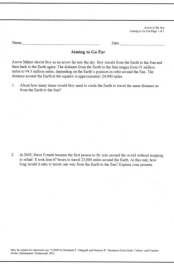

strategies other than actually measuring to determine congruency and other relationships. For instance, students should be encouraged to justify through folding with their patty or wax paper, such as proving triangles are congruent by using reflection symmetry.

Students study properties of basic geometry shapes in Questions 3, 4, and 6, such as isosceles triangles and quadrilaterals that are kites. Students more than likely have encountered all of these shapes, with the possible exception of a kite, but will not necessarily be familiar with properties needed to justify that the figure is indeed that shape. Although students may have experienced playing with kites, they are less likely to be familiar with how kites are derived or defined geometrically. A kite is a quadrilateral with two distinct pairs of adjacent congruent sides; after students have explored these quadrilaterals in their outlines, teachers should lead a discussion to help students develop a definition for this figure.

Growing in Stature

This investigation provides an opportunity for students to examine the impact on similarity between figures when they are stretched or distorted in one dimension and not in the other. Throughout this investigation, students are expected to build the figures physically using square tiles; if teachers do not have access to such manipulatives, students could draw figures on one-inch square grid paper.

Teachers should monitor students as they complete this task because many middle-grades students may believe that similarity is just "figures with the same shape," which is an incomplete definition. If a shape grows in only one dimension, then a figure is not automatically similar to itself because it has been distorted. So, students need to experience making different shapes to witness this distortion and to focus on the relationships required in similar figures (corresponding side lengths proportional and corresponding angles congruent).

In Questions 1–3, the given figures are not similar because the stretch factor is applied in only one dimension. Such changes are labeled *scale changes*. If students struggle to determine whether the figures are similar or not, teachers might have students build a 2×2 square and then triple only one dimension to obtain a 2×6 rectangle. Students likely do not have any difficulty recognizing that the original square and the rectangle are *not* similar. Just as the square and rectangle are not similar when only one dimension is stretched, the various figure people are not similar because the figures are stretched in only one direction.

In Questions 4–6, the given figures are similar because the stretch factor is applied in both dimensions. Such changes are labeled *size changes*. In these cases, the ratio of the areas of a figure to the original is the square of the size change factor. Last, the challenge question provides an extension to this investigation related to the ratio of the areas when figures are similar.

Aiming to Go Far

In this investigation, students have an opportunity to work with basic distance facts related to the Earth and the Sun. The brief nature of this investigation makes it possible to consider using it as a warm-up problem for the day or as an extended homework assignment.

Students often have difficulty comprehending such large distances. In Question 1, students compare the distance from the Earth to the Sun to the distance around the Earth; they would need to circle the Earth more than 3,600 times to approach the distance from the Earth to the Sun.

Steve Fossett was an adventurer who attempted to be the first to complete numerous solo flights under different conditions. In 2005, he was the first to circumnavigate the globe solo without refueling (www.msnbc.msn.com/id/7075972/). It can be informative for students to compare the flight time from the Earth to the Sun if they traveled as fast as Steve Fossett did. Students should be expected to convert the number of hours to a measure that is easier to comprehend, likely the number of years. Interested students might investigate other distance records and report about them as extensions to this task.

Reference

McDermott, Gerald. 1974. *Arrow to the Sun: A Pueblo Indian Tale*. New York: Viking.

CHAPTER 23

Buffalo Woman

About the Resource

Cultural Index			Mathematics Index	
Amenable	**Beneficial**	**Compelling**	**Explicit**	**Implicit**
		✓		✓

This Native American story is based on tales from Plains Tribes who depended on the buffalo for food, clothing, and shelter. When a hunter falls asleep, he awakens to find that a young woman has been sent by the Buffalo Nation to be his wife. Although he loves her and the son they have together, the hunter's family makes fun of the young woman because she smells like an animal. One day while the hunter is away, the woman decides to return to her own people (the buffalo). When the hunter arrives at the Buffalo Nation, he must identify his wife and son, or else he will lose both them and his own life.

Cultural Group: Native American and Indigenous Peoples

Mathematical Focus

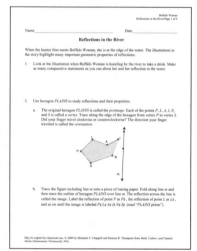

Investigation: Reflections in the River

- drawing reflection images across a line
- properties of reflections, including angle measures and distance from the reflection line
- measuring angles

Investigation: Tipi Sizes

- circumference and area of circles
- finding arc length and area of circular sectors
- building cones from circular sectors

Commentary About the Investigations

The investigations in this chapter can be completed independent of each other. For Reflections in the River, students need access to protractors and rulers. For Tipi Sizes, students need scissors, rulers, and compasses.

Reflections in the River

This investigation provides students an opportunity to explore properties of reflections. The illustrations in the story are quite beautiful; in particular, the illustration of Buffalo Woman kneeling along the water's edge highlights the mirror image aspect of reflections. So, in Question 1 students simply make informal observations about this illustration.

In Question 2, students begin to explore properties of reflections using a concave hexagon. We chose a concave figure rather than a convex one so that it would be easier for students to recognize corresponding points between a preimage (the original) and the image (the reflection). Depending on students' prior experiences, teachers may need to spend some time at the beginning of the investigation addressing the vocabulary of *preimage*, *image*, and *reflecting line* as well as the conventional use of primes to label image points.

There are many ways for students to draw the reflection image. They can use tracing paper (or patty paper) to trace the preimage and the reflecting line; then, students can fold along the reflecting line, look at the outline of the preimage through the paper, and trace the image. Or if available, students can use a MIRA, a commercial manipulative used to study transformations. They should place the MIRA along the reflecting line and trace the image that is viewed through the MIRA. Alternatively, teachers could modify the figure and have students build a figure (preimage) using pattern blocks, build the image with pattern blocks, and then trace around the outline of both the preimage and the image. If teachers have access to Geometer's Sketchpad and enough computers, students could complete the investigation with this tool. However, it is useful for students to have the kinesthetic experience of drawing the image on their own at least once; so, teachers might have students draw or build images for a few examples before having them use Geometer's Sketchpad to draw the image and measure corresponding parts.

In Questions 2a and 2c, students should recognize that reflections reverse the orientation of a figure. As students draw and measure segments and measure distances from a point to the reflecting line, they should begin to realize that the reflecting line bisects the segment joining a preimage and its corresponding image (Questions 2d and 2e). In contrast, corresponding angle measures are congruent (Question 3). Question 3b highlights a type of angle that students have likely not experienced previously. This angle is neither acute nor obtuse because its measure is more than 180°; to help students realize this, have students place their finger on segment $\overline{LA}$ and then rotate their finger to segment $\overline{AI}$ while staying inside the hexagon. Students should realize that they went beyond a straight line and so measured more than 180°. If students measure the exterior obtuse angle $\angle LAI$, then the measure of this angle and the measure of the angle interior to the hexagon must sum to 360° because the two angles surround a point. The interior angle at vertex A is called a *reflexive angle*.

Perhaps students have previously studied properties related to the sum of the interior angle measures in a polygon; if so, they should know that this sum in a hexagon is 720°. Given that students will have determined the measures for 5 of the 6 angles, they could use the sum and the 5 known angle measures to determine the measure of the interior reflexive angle. If students use both approaches, they could compare to see that they get the same measure.

Question 5 provides an extension task for students. All the properties of reflections that students studied in Questions 2 and 3 still hold when the reflecting line intersects the preimage. However, it is sometimes more difficult for students to draw the image in this situation. Teachers will need to determine whether this task is appropriate for the majority of students in their class.

Because there are other examples for which the illustration shows the preimage and the reflection image, in Question 6 students return to the book to find other examples. For the final question in this investigation, students are able to design their own geometric design. If there is access to pattern blocks, teachers may consider having students use this manipulative to build their designs.

Tipi Sizes

In this investigation, students have an opportunity to examine the circumference and area of circles and sectors of circles. These sectors are used to build cones to simulate the construction of tipis.

Students should start with several circles of the same size. In the task, students fold the circle so there are 8 sections. We chose this number because it is relatively easy to fold the circle in this way; teachers can certainly have students fold the circle to obtain sectors of other sizes. As students cut out sectors of different sizes, they are able to re-shape the remaining sectors into cones. As more of a circle is cut out, its cone will have greater height but a smaller base.

Teachers need to determine whether students have had prior experience working with circumference and area formulas for circles. In this task, students are simply expected to use the formulas; development of the formulas should have occurred previously. The purpose of Question 2 is for students to realize that the arc of the sector forms the circumference of the base of the cone. The arc length of the sector is determined as a fraction of the circumference of the original circle. When students determine both the arc length and the circumference of the base of the cone, they should leave their answers in terms of π so that the relationship between arc length and circumference of the base is more apparent. Because of measurement error, it is not likely that answers will completely agree, but they should be close enough to support discussion about why they are so close, and in fact, the same.

Students should be able to use their work in Question 2 to determine a process for finding the lateral area of the cone. This lateral area corresponds to the area of hides used to construct a tipi.

Reference

Goble, Paul. 1984. *Buffalo Woman*. New York: Aladdin.

CHAPTER 24

First Day in Grapes

About the Resource

This delightful story depicts the adventures of a young Mexican boy, Chico, who attends new schools throughout the year as his family travels from one migrant camp to another to pick fruits and veg-

Cultural Index			Mathematics Index	
Amenable	**B**eneficial	**C**ompelling	Explicit	Implicit
		✓	✓	

etables. Chico has many *first days* in schools—first days in oranges, first days in garlic, or first days in tomatoes—all based on the crop his family picks at each camp. Being a new student who speaks Spanish, Chico is sometimes bullied by older kids, and so he often dislikes school. However, at Chico's school related to the first day in grapes, the situation is different. His teacher likes him and his classmates recognize his excellent math skills. They encourage him to participate in the upcoming Math Fair. When bullies approach Chico at lunch, he responds bravely and finds a creative way to deflect potential trouble. Chico's story is a reminder that we all possess inner courage if we only learn to use it.

Cultural Group: Latino

Mathematical Focus

 ### Investigation: Mind-Full-Paper-Less Counting

- mental mathematics
- computation skills, including strategies

 ### Investigation: Crates of Grapes

- computations
- writing algebraic expressions for inequalities
- writing and solving algebraic relationships
- problem solving

Commentary About the Investigations

These two investigations build from ideas noted in the story. They can be assigned independent of each other. Stopwatches are needed for the game in Mind-Full-Paper-Less Counting, one for each group of three students.

Mind-Full-Paper-Less Counting

This investigation provides opportunities for students to perform number operations mentally and enhance their skills in this area. Middle-grades students often need to practice their operation skills. Sometimes, as they expand their experiences with scientific and graphing calculators, they become careless with basic operations. In addition, many curricula provide only minimal opportunities for students to engage in mental mathematics or to estimate answers to problems. Although we strongly advocate for appropriate use of calculators in the mathematics classroom, we do value and believe that students should know their operation facts and be able to conduct mental computations in an appropriate time interval.

The purpose of Questions 1–7 is twofold: (1) to have students compute a number of problems mentally and (2) to have students engage in a conversation about possible strategies to use with mental mathematics. After students have completed some mental mathematics problems, it is useful to have them discuss possible strategies with their peers. As students talk about different approaches used, they build their repertoire of mental strategies for future use.

The final task in this investigation is a game. Students should work in groups of three, with each pair of students competing while the third person keeps time. At each round, three problems are completed. Teachers might flash these problems via an overhead projector, computer projector, or through some other device. Students can write solutions on paper or on small white boards. Another strategy is to use plastic sheet protectors with dry-erase markers: put a blank sheet of paper inside the sheet protector, and students write on the sheet protector with a dry-erase marker. Alternatively, teachers might place problems on index cards and distribute the index cards to the groups; students shuffle and draw the cards for each round from the deck. Teachers can focus the problems on skills that are a particular concern for the students in the class.

Crates of Grapes

This investigation provides an opportunity for students to use situations from the story to solve inequality relationships and write those relationships symbolically. Middle-grades students may have often solved or graphed an inequality without thinking about contextual situations in which such inequalities might arise. So, in these problems, the inequalities (Questions 1 and 2) arise from problems related to situations described in the story.

Questions 3, 4, and 5 contain situations involving equality related to contexts from the story. Students might solve these problems by first writing algebraic equations. Or, they might attempt some type of guess-and-check approach. In each case, they must deal with more than one condition at the same time.

Questions 6 and 7 enable students to consider the possible wages for workers involved in picking grapes. The actual wages received can vary depending on the type of grape and the location; the values used in Question 6 are based on wages for raisin grapes from California (http://migration.ucdavis.edu/cf/files/conference_may_2008/martin_mason-californias_farm_labor_market-the_case_of_raisin_grapes.pdf). Some grapes seem to be packaged in crates, others in trays. Although Questions 1–5 use the term *crates* to connect with the story, in Question 6 the term *trays* is used as synonymous with crates.

Question 7 highlights the markup that often occurs from the farm to the grocery store. Students need to realize that the wages in Question 6 are for a 20-pound tray and the price in Question 7 is for a *single* pound. To determine the percent increase, the two measures need to be based on the same unit, either a single pound or 20 pounds. This problem also provides a context for discussion about why prices might rise from the farm to the grocery store. There are various processors who handle the grapes between the farm and the store and each adds some costs to the process.

If students are in an area with farmers' markets, teachers might have them compare prices of different fruits and vegetables at a farmer's market to the prices of the same products in a grocery store. Also, if there are farms nearby, teachers might attempt to check with local farmers to determine the wages paid for harvesting the crops in that area and then make comparisons to the prices of those crops in the grocery store.

Reference

Perez, L. King. 2002. *First Day in Grapes*. New York: Lee & Low Books.

CHAPTER 25

Harvesting Hope: The Story of Cesar Chavez

About the Resource

Cultural Index			Mathematics Index	
Amenable	Beneficial	Compelling	Explicit	Implicit
		✓		✓

This Pura Belpré Honor book chronicles the life of Cesar Chavez, a Latino farmworker and civil rights labor leader, from his early years as a soft-spoken, shy boy to his labor activism as an adult. Chavez was often teased at school, and he dropped out after the eighth grade to work full-time in the farm fields of southern California. Because he was a problem solver, he began a crusade for nonviolent change that would improve the working conditions for migrant farm laborers. His work ultimately led to the creation of the National Farm Workers Association, the first successful farmworkers' union in American history. Through his union efforts, groundbreaking laws for the protection of farmworkers were passed in California and throughout the country.

Cultural Group: Latino

Mathematical Focus

 Investigation: Walk for the Cause

- computations with natural numbers
- finding percent, including percent increase
- problem solving

 Investigation: Factor in the Farmers

- percent, including percent increase or decrease
- creating and interpreting graphical displays

Commentary About the Investigations

Students can complete these two investigations independent of each other; they will need access to the Internet for part of Factor in the Farmers. Teachers may want to refer to the following websites to view other details about Chavez's life: www.chavez foundation.org and www.nationalchavezcenter.org.

Walk for the Cause

This investigation highlights an important event in the life of Cesar Chavez, namely the march that he led to seek government help to improve working conditions for farmworkers. Question 1 provides an opportunity for students to focus on important aspects of this march. Students are likely to be astonished at the percent increase in Question 1b and perhaps think they have made an error. Teachers should help students realize that 10,000 is slightly more than 147 times the size of the initial number, 68, so such a large percent makes sense.

Questions 2 and 3 extend the context from the farmworkers' march to many other marches that individuals complete for a particular cause. In Question 2, the march parameters are provided for students; their work in Question 2 should serve as a guide when they plan the conditions for their own march in Question 3. The data in the table in Question 2c lead to a rational function of the form $y = \frac{k}{x}$ where k is a constant. As students graph these data, they have an opportunity to work with a function that is not linear. Middle-grades students should have experiences with a wide variety of functions, including nonlinear functions, prior to their formal work in algebra.

In Question 3, students plan conditions for a march related to a cause of their own choice. Students might actually consider conducting and participating in a walk-a-thon for that cause. If the local community hosts walk-a-thons for major causes (e.g., Komen walk for a breast cancer cure), teachers might connect aspects of Question 3 to similar conditions related to the community walk-a-thon.

Factor in the Farmers

The U.S. Department of Agriculture's (USDA) website (www.agcensus.usda.gov/ Publications/2002/) contains a wealth of data about farms in the United States over time, by state as well as for the country as a whole. In this investigation, students explore some of these data for California as a connection to the story, for the entire United States, and then for their own state. Questions 1 and 2 provide an opportunity for students to explore the change in the number of farms in both California and the country; in Question 3, students make the same comparisons for the farm situation in their own state using data from the USDA website. Given the large numbers involved here, it is likely more informative and meaningful to compare numbers in terms of percents rather than absolute changes in the number of farms. The actual difference is a large number that is often hard to comprehend; a percent change provides better insight into whether the change is relatively large or small.

In Question 4, students should speculate about reasons for the decline in the number of farms. Some possible explanations are the difficulty of the work, the high cost of farming in relation to the income, and the consolidation of farms by large corporations. In fact, although the number of farms and the total acreage in farms has declined, the size of farms has increased, often because farms are now controlled by large food corporations.

Question 5 gives students an opportunity to determine appropriate graphical displays for a set of data. Although there are several options for students, it is probably most beneficial to display the data as a bar graph or as a circle graph. Because the data set in the table represents the whole and no farm is in more than one category, a circle graph is an appropriate display. When students construct bar graphs, they may need some assistance to determine an appropriate scale for the y-axis given the large numbers for the farms.

Reference

Krull, Kathleen. 2004. *Harvesting Hope: The Story of Cesar Chavez.* San Diego: Harcourt.

CHAPTER 26

Abuela's Weave

About the Resource

Esperanza and her grandmother, Abuela, weave in the traditional Guatemalan manner, with vibrant colors and intricate folk patterns. As the Fiesta de Pueblos in the city of Guate approaches, they make

Cultural Index			Mathematics Index	
Amenable	**B**eneficial	**C**ompelling	**E**xplicit	**I**mplicit
		✓	✓	

plans to travel from their village to the city to sell their goods at the marketplace. Esperanza is concerned that the items she wove with her grandmother will not be able to compete with items woven via machines. However, everyone is enchanted with the colors and patterns in their goods; they sell all they brought to the market and return to their village with plans to start weaving for the next market day.

Cultural Group: Latino

Mathematical Focus

 Investigation: Fair Trade at the Marketplace

- computations, including with percent
- working with rates
- problem solving

 Investigation: Patterns in the Weave

- describing geometric designs
- lines of symmetry
- rotation (turn) symmetry

Commentary About the Investigations

The two investigations in this chapter can be completed independent of each other. Teachers may want to download pictures from several websites that illustrate the vibrancy of the color and patterns in Guatemalan weaving.

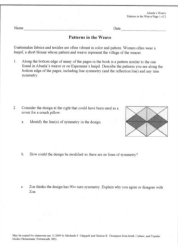

Fair Trade at the Marketplace

In this investigation, students have an opportunity to explore the possibilities of selling materials at a marketplace as a way to raise money to support a family. In Question 1, students simply determine the income received if the given items with the specified quantities are sold. The quantities in the table were constructed using the illustrations in the book as a guide to the items Esperanza had to sell. Several websites describe Guatemalan textiles and handcrafts; we based our prices on items for sale at www.littlemangoimports.com.

In Question 2, students work with rates, specifically the cost per purse or per group of 3 purses. It is not uncommon for markets to offer a discount when a buyer purchases multiple quantities of an item. In this instance, students must think about how many groups of 3 are formed in each case; the number of groups determines the multiplier of $90 for large purses or $80 for small purses. Question 2d is a challenge problem; students have the answer—the total income—but need to determine a type of purchase (the number of purses of each size sold and the condition of sale, individually or in a group of 3). If students have access to spreadsheet software, this would be a good task for exploration with such computer programs.

Question 3 provides an opportunity for students to engage in a task related to social responsibility and awareness. Many artisans in third-world countries struggle to support their family and lift themselves out of poverty when they are forced to sell their wares at an extremely low price in order to be competitive. Consequently, Fair Trade Federations have arisen to help artisans form cooperatives so that fair prices are established (see www.coloresdelpueblo.org/index.htm and http://moonflowerenterprises .com/products.php?id=006). Students may be quite surprised to realize that $5.25 *per day* was a fair trade wage in Guatemala in 2007, given the current minimum wages in the United States (http://educationandmore.wordpress.com/2007/10/02/daily-living-wage/). Students should realize the total income and quantities sold in Questions 1 and 2 exceed Fair Trade wages by quite a bit. As an extension, teachers might want to have students look in local grocery stores to find items for sale that indicate they are sold as part of a global Fair Trade Federation; one item commonly found for sale under these conditions is coffee.

Patterns in the Weave

The tasks in this investigation give students an opportunity to explore and describe geometric designs found in Guatemalan weaving. Students will need to look carefully at the pages in the book to describe the symmetries found in the designs along the bottom edge of the pages; although eight pages have a design along the edge, there are only four distinct designs (Question 1).

In Question 2, students investigate the symmetry of a given design and consider how it can be modified to preserve or change the symmetries. In each case, students must consider how color interacts within the design to enhance or inhibit symmetries. That is, students cannot focus just on shape but must also consider color when determining whether or not there is a particular type of symmetry.

For Question 3, students need access to pattern blocks or some other type of manipulative with color, preferably a manipulative that also contains various shapes. Students should be encouraged to build their (two-dimensional) designs physically before transferring their designs to grid paper.

For the final question, students need access to the Internet to explore Guatemalan products of interest to them. In addition to looking at the patterns, students might also consider the prices of these objects. For example, the price of a huipil can vary greatly from $20 to several hundred dollars.

Reference

Castañeda, Omar S. 1993. *Abuela's Weave*. New York: Lee & Low Books.

CHAPTER 27

Piñatas & Smiling Skeletons: Celebrating Mexican Festivals

About the Resource

Cultural Index			Mathematics Index	
Amenable	**B**eneficial	**C**ompelling	Explicit	Implicit
		✓		✓

This book is a compilation of history and traditions related to six important Mexican festivals, including The Virgin of Guadalupe, Christmas, Carnaval, Corpus Christi, Independence Day, and the Day of the Dead. Throughout, the book discusses how distinctly Mexican traditions resulted from the blending of traditions from indigenous peoples and Spanish explorers. These traditions are practiced today not only by those living in Mexico but by Mexicans who have migrated to the United States. The book is richly illustrated; individual pages can be used separately if teachers are not interested in reading the entire book.

Cultural Group: Latino

Mathematical Focus

 Investigation: Piñatas and Aguinaldos

- volume of a cylinder
- lateral surface area of a cylinder

 Investigation: Mexican Sweets

- number operations, particularly with fractions
- measurements, particularly those associated with cooking
- scaling recipes up or down

Commentary About the Investigations

These investigations can be completed independent of each other. For Piñatas and Aguinaldos, teachers will need to collect or have students bring to class the cardboard rolls from toilet paper or from paper towels. Also, for this investigation, teachers may

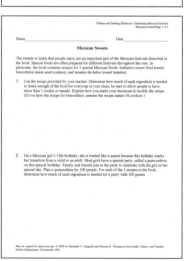

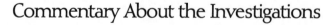

want to have available a sample piñata, one either purchased from a store or constructed by decorating a small shoe box.

Piñatas and Aguinaldos

Many students are likely to be familiar with piñatas and to have seen them in a party store or in a section of a discount store selling party decorations. This investigation uses piñatas as a motivation to explore lateral surface area and volume of cylinders. Teachers may want to purchase an inexpensive piñata and bring it to class. If so, we encourage teachers to fill the piñata with candy, then show students a single piece of the candy and have them estimate the number of pieces that the piñata can hold. In essence, teachers are having students make estimates about volume based on a nonstandard unit.

Students may or may not have had previous experiences dealing with surface area or volume of a cylinder. If students have previously studied the area formula for a circle, then teachers can help them think of a cylinder as a set of circles stacked on top of each other. Thus, the formula for the volume of a cylinder is $V = \pi r^2 h$, where r is the radius and h is the height; this formula becomes the basis for the work in Question 1.

Because piñatas are typically filled with candy or small toys, their size is often indicated in terms of the number of children that the piñata can serve. To help students translate the volume per child of the piñata (Question 1b) into a meaningful quantity, in Question 1c students are encouraged to fold a rectangle into a small box whose volume is equivalent to the volume per child. This visual can be a powerful way to help students conceptualize a particular volume.

To help students make sense of the formula for the lateral surface area of a cylinder ($A = 2\pi rh$), teachers might begin by bringing in cans of vegetables. The label on the can represents the lateral area; when the label is removed and flattened, it is a rectangle. Students should know how to find the area of a rectangle; they likely will need help to realize that one dimension of the rectangle is the circumference of the can. This situation is analogous to finding the lateral area of a cardboard insert for a roll of toilet paper or paper towels. The paper needed to wrap the cardboard insert should extend 2 inches beyond the edges in order to tie the ends in a decorative manner and ensure that candy stays inside the roll.

The website provided in Question 5 gives students an opportunity to explore other aspects of piñatas. After students construct problems, peers solve those problems. If a problem is unclear, the original writer of the problem should be expected to revise it so it makes sense.

Mexican Sweets

Mexican festivals typically involve many sweets that people enjoy. So, in this investigation, students have an opportunity to modify a recipe to serve all the students in their class. As a prerequisite to scaling the recipe up or down to create more or less, students need to think about the amount that each person in the class will eat. Then, based on the quantity the recipe makes, students can determine the scale factor needed to modify the recipe (Question 1).

The quinceañera is an important milestone in the life of a Mexican girl. All families, regardless of socioeconomic status, plan some type of celebration to honor the girl on this special day that marks her transition from a child to an adult. Again, to modify the recipes to serve 100 people (Question 2), students first need to consider how many of each sweet a person will eat in order to modify the recipe appropriately.

Teachers can certainly extend this investigation by having students bring in other Mexican recipes from a cookbook or from the Web. Or, students could bring in favorite recipes representing their own culture to have an international food festival within the class.

Reference

Harris, Zoe, and Suzanne Williams. 1998. *Piñatas & Smiling Skeletons: Celebrating Mexican Festivals*. Berkeley, CA: Pacific View Press.

CHAPTER 28

Issunbōshi

About the Resource

This folktale describes the adventures of Issunbōshi, a Japanese boy who is just one inch tall from birth. After reaching manhood, he leaves his parents' house to enter the services of the emperor and

Cultural Index			Mathematics Index	
Amenable	**B**eneficial	**C**ompelling	**E**xplicit	**I**mplicit
		✓		✓

becomes the favored bodyguard for the Prime Minister's daughter, Miyuki. When Issunbōshi saves Miyuki from an attack, he is rewarded with a wish—to become a full-sized man warrior. He is honored by the Prime Minister and invited to marry his daughter; the two marry and live happily thereafter.

Cultural Group: Asian and Pacific Islanders

Mathematical Focus

 Investigation: Living Life One Inch Tall

- measurement, specifically finding lengths
- using and comparing ratios
- problem solving

 Investigation: Timing a Journey

- measurement, including rates
- problem solving

Commentary About the Investigations

These investigations provide opportunities for students to explore ratio and proportions by considering the relative size of an object to a person's height. Teachers might want to bring objects into class for students to measure, such as a rice bowl, chopsticks, and other everyday objects (e.g., toothbrush, hairbrush, fork, plate).

Although the two investigations can be completed independent of each other, Timing a Journey uses information about height collected in Living Life One Inch Tall.

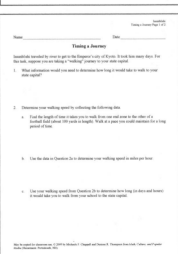

If teachers have difficulty finding a copy of the book, a version of the story can be found at legends-folktales.blogspot.com/2007/10/tiny-finger-issunboshi.html.

Living Life One Inch Tall

The tasks in this investigation are open-ended and provide many opportunities for students to focus on aspects of interest to them. In particular, in Questions 3 and 5, students need to compare their heights to everyday objects of their choice, with some objects larger in size (Question 3) and some smaller in size (Question 5). In fact, teachers might consider assigning Questions 3a and 3b as homework so that students bring the dimensions to class prior to reading the story and completing the remainder of the investigation.

Question 6 can be quite challenging for students. A student who is 48 inches tall is 48 times the height of Issunbōshi, so to draw the 2 figures in perspective means that the ratio of their heights is 1:48. Clearly students could tape sheets of paper together in order to draw the figures. But the restriction of the problem is to draw the figures on a single sheet of paper. Hence, Issunbōshi will need to be drawn less than half an inch in height. In fact, if Issunbōshi is drawn $\frac{1}{8}$ inch tall then a 48-inch-tall student would be drawn 6 inches tall. Students will need to use their problem-solving skills to be successful on this problem.

Timing a Journey

In this investigation, students have an opportunity to collect data through some physical activity. If the middle school is structured in teams, mathematics teachers might work with physical education teachers who have their students collect data about the time needed to walk a football field (Question 2a).

Students might need help converting their data to speed in miles per hour. An efficient approach is to use unit analysis, a strategy that students may have studied in science class. If students have not seen this approach previously, teachers might consider introducing it to students as it has important connections to ideas related to fraction multiplication. For instance, suppose a student walks a football field in 2 minutes. Then, the student's speed can be found as follows:

$$\frac{100 \text{ yards}}{2 \text{ min}} \cdot \frac{60 \text{ min}}{1 \text{ h}} \cdot \frac{1 \text{ mi}}{1,760 \text{ yards}} \approx 1.7 \text{ mi/h}$$

When using this approach, students need to include units with each conversion rate. Then, students can see how the units multiply and divide so they obtain the desired units upon completion of the computation.

If students completed Living Life One Inch Tall, they determined their height in comparison to Issunbōshi's height; if students did not complete this investigation, they will need to measure their height before continuing with Question 3b. For middle-grades students who are 4 feet tall (48 inches), the ratio of their height to Issunbōshi's is 48 to 1. So, it should take Issunbōshi about 48 times as long to travel the distance from their school to the state capital.

Reference

Goodman, Robert, and Robert A. Spicer (Adapted by). 1974. *Issunbōshi*. Aiea, HI: Island Heritage.

CHAPTER 29

Munna and the Grain of Rice

About the Resource

Cultural Index			Mathematics Index	
Amenable	**B**eneficial	**C**ompelling	**E**xplicit	**I**mplicit
		✓	✓	

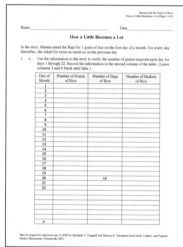

This story is one in a delightful collection of Indian children's folktales. Munna, the elephant keeper's daughter who never had a chance to attend school, is quite observant and generous. When she sees her people starving due to a famine in the kingdom, she grows concerned. Responding to Munna's act of honesty one day, the Raja decides to reward her. She slyly asks for one grain of rice on the first day of a month; for every day thereafter, she asks for twice the amount as on the previous day. In the end, Munna humbles the unwise and unjust Raja by emptying all his storehouses of rice. He learns to share with the people of his kingdom so that everyone can eat.

Cultural Group: Asian and Pacific Islanders

Mathematical Focus

 ### Investigation: How a Little Becomes a Lot

- problem solving using exponential growth patterns
- writing algebraic expressions for exponential growth patterns
- representing patterns in tabular and graphical forms

 ### Investigation: Weighty Rice

- calculating weight measurements
- using ratios and proportions
- comparing units of measurement

Commentary About the Investigations

Although the two investigations can be completed independent of each other, Weighty Rice will likely make more sense if students have first completed How a Little Becomes a Lot. Students need access at least to scientific calculators for these activities; the focus should be on problem solving and looking for patterns, not on long computations by hand. Teachers will need small bags of rice from the grocery store for Weighty Rice.

How a Little Becomes a Lot

In the elementary grades, students often work on additive relationships. Consequently, they may not realize how fast multiplicative relationships can grow. This investigation provides an opportunity for students to work on doubling relationships, which lead to exponential growth patterns.

All students should be able to complete the rows in the table for specific days, whether the number is in terms of grains of rice, bags of rice, or baskets of rice (Questions 1a, 2a, and 3a, respectively). However, students may need some guidance to rewrite these quantities as exponential expressions (Questions 1b, 2c, and 3c), particularly if they fail to realize that the numbers are powers of 2. In order to write a general expression, students need to relate the power of 2 to the day number. These questions provide good connections to algebraic expressions with variables, but students may need some discussion if they have not had prior experiences with problems of this type.

Many middle-grades students only experience graphs of linear relationships. So, it is beneficial for them to graph exponential relationships as expected in Question 4. Teachers should engage students in discussions about how this graph differs from graphs of linear functions with which they are likely already familiar.

Questions 6 and 7 serve as additional challenge and extension questions for those students who are ready and prepared for such a challenge. In Question 6, most students should be able to find the total number of grains of rice received as a function of the day; writing that expression algebraically may be a bit more difficult. However, if students have completed the challenges in Question 2c and 3c, they are likely to be better prepared to tackle this problem. So, teachers might want to let students work in small groups and attempt to find a solution.

Question 7 is designed to compare and contrast doubling and tripling relationships. Because students have experience from the doubling relationship in Question 1, teachers might begin by asking students how many days they think would be needed before Munna would receive one million grains of rice. Students are likely to be surprised at how much faster one million grains are received when tripling rather than when doubling.

Weighty Rice

In this investigation, students have an opportunity to explore the possible weight of the rice that Munna received. Students can use the given information in the first problem to determine the number of grains of rice in one of Munna's small bags. To determine the weight of this bag (Question 2c), students do some investigative work using a typical bag of rice from a grocery store.

Students need to work together to determine some effective ways, other than actual counting, to determine the number of grains of rice in the bag from the store (Question 2b) in order to compare this to the number of grains in Munna's bag. Perhaps students might pour the rice onto a small section of paper and count the number of grains in that section before multiplying by the number of sections of paper containing rice. Once students have an estimate of the number of grains of rice in their bag, they can compare that number to the 32,768 grains of rice in Munna's bag. The weight of 1 small bag of rice for Munna is then given by the following expression:

$$\frac{32,768}{\text{number of grains of rice in their bag}} \bullet \text{weight of their bag of rice}$$

As students attempt to determine the weight of the rice Munna received on day 28, they need to remember that Munna received rice on that day in baskets, not in bags. Students can refer to their work on How a Little Becomes a Lot to figure the number of bags in a basket in order to determine the weight of a basket. Still, this number is likely to be hard for students to understand. So, in Question 4, students compare the weight of the rice to the weight of an equivalent number of middle-grades students. Teachers could determine a weight range for students at their grade level from national charts prior to beginning this task.

From a similar literature resource, titled *A Grain of Rice* (Pittman 1986, Bantam Skylark), three other previously published investigations that complement those presented in this chapter are provided on the CD-ROM. As an additional extension, teachers may want to investigate other facts about rice from rice-producing countries. One useful website is www.mapsofworld.com/world-top-ten/countries-with-most-rice-producing-countries.html.

Reference

Somaiah, Rosemarie (Retold by). 2006. "Munna and the Grain of Rice." In *Indian Children's Favourite Stories*, 8–15. Tokyo: Tuttle.

CHAPTER 30

The Adventures of Marco Polo

About the Resource

This book shares remarkable tales of Marco Polo, the famous thirteenth-century adventurer who claimed to have traveled from his homeland of Venice, Italy to the court of Kublai Khan in far-

	Cultural Index		Mathematics Index	
Amenable	**B**eneficial	**C**ompelling	**E**xplicit	**I**mplicit
		✓	✓	

eastern China. Marco's travels with his father and uncle spanned a period of twenty-four years; during this time, Marco traveled farther than any previous European. While imprisoned in Genoa during a war between Italian city-states, Marco shared his tales with Rustichello of Pisa, who helped bring them to life in a book. Marco's tales share perspectives of life among the Mongols and the Chinese, a life far different from anything that most Europeans at the time could comprehend.

Cultural Group: Asian and Pacific Islanders

Mathematical Focus

 Investigation: Great Are the Numbers

- comparisons with large numbers
- problem solving
- area and perimeter applications

 Investigation: Postal Relay

- algebraic patterns
- networks, including traversability

Commentary About the Investigations

These investigations are based on different scenarios from the book. They can be completed independent of each other. Depending on time, teachers may choose to read only one or two chapters at a time rather than read the entire book. Teachers might also consider reading chapters over several days before beginning the investigations so that students develop a sense of the context of the story.

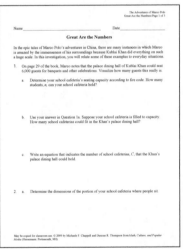

In the 1980s, there was a television miniseries based on the adventures of Marco Polo. Although there was a 2007 film about Marco's adventures, we were not particularly impressed with this movie.

Great Are the Numbers

In this investigation, students explore problems that help them understand the immenseness of Kublai Khan's surroundings. In particular, the focus is on the chapter "In the Court of Kublai Khan," which reports Kublai Khan's living quarters and daily lifestyle. Marco Polo seemed to be in awe of the vast numbers of people and things that were a normal part of Khan's life. So, in the investigation students relate these seemingly huge numbers to their everyday situations.

In Question 1a, students envision what 6,000 dinner guests would look like by relating this number to the number of students their school cafeteria could hold. Students will need to think of the capacity of their cafeteria as a unit (divisor) to determine how many cafeterias are necessary to hold 6,000 guests. For example, the fire code capacity of a typical school cafeteria might be 300 students; in this case, students should realize that 20 cafeterias would be needed to seat Khan's 6,000 guests. Problems such as this one can help students understand large numbers by relating them to a common context with which they are already familiar. Students then think more generally about this situation and derive an equation to represent it (Question 1c).

In the next task (Question 2), students think about how large a space is needed to hold 6,000 guests. This is not unreasonable because many hotel ballrooms can seat several thousand people. For this question, students will again need to use the cafeteria dimensions as a unit to provide a good estimate as to the size of Khan's dining palace. Students do a similar comparison in Question 3 for 40,000 guests; they can use places like stadiums or large concert halls to get a sense of the numbers.

In Question 4, students think about the arrangement of square dinner tables for a more manageable number of tables, specifically 400. Here, students are applying and comparing area versus perimeter. If the tables have an area of 1 square unit (i.e., the tables are 1 unit on a side), then the area of the arrangement of the tables is always 400 square units (Question 4a). However, the perimeter changes as the dimensions of the arrangement change; because only 1 person sits on a side, the perimeter corresponds to the number of guests possible (Question 4b). In Question 4d, students compare costs based on area versus perimeter and determine the most cost-effective payment per arrangement.

The final problem provides an opportunity for students to think about large numbers in an inequality relationship. They can determine both the minimum number of types of gifts as well as the minimum number of gifts that each of the 5,000 elephants and camels bring to the ruler.

Postal Relay

The postal system is described in the chapter "In the Court of Kublai Khan." The system accommodated the delivery of ordinary messages via foot as well as the delivery of more time-sensitive messages via horseback. Because messengers were relieved every 3 miles, a message could travel without interruption from its starting point to its delivery point. In Question 1, students build a table to describe the distance remaining after n messengers have handled a message. If teachers have access to graphing calculators, students should graph the equation that gives the distance the message has left to travel after n messengers have transported it. This linear graph has a negative slope; students should recognize that the y-intercept represents the total distance to be traveled and the slope is the distance traveled by each messenger. So, each additional messenger reduces the distance by 3 miles. Although the actual x-intercept is 66.7, the contextual nature of the problem demands that 67 messengers help transport the message.

Questions 2 and 3 provide an opportunity for students to explore a topic in graph theory, namely networks. This is an important topic in many real-world situations as businesses want to ensure that a delivery person does not travel the same road more than once. Gas costs and employee time raise delivery costs, so being efficient in travel is important.

The study of networks began when Euler tried to solve the famous Königsberg bridge problem. The city of Königsberg was located on both sides of a river in which there were 2 islands. Seven bridges joined the islands to each other and to the city on both sides of the river. Euler tried to determine if it was possible to take a walk and cross each of the 7 bridges once and only once. (See http://en.wikipedia.org/wiki/K%C3%B6nigsberg_bridge_problem.)

Students can try to traverse or travel the figures in Question 2 without traveling a road more than once. They should realize that a city with an odd number of roads originating from it must be the starting or ending point of a path. So, a path can only be traversable if all the cities have an even number of roads or if there are only two cities with an odd number of roads.

Reference

Freedman, Russell. 2006. *The Adventures of Marco Polo*. New York: Arthur A. Levine.

SECTION **IV**

Internet Resources

This section contains eleven investigations based on three Internet resources; each of these resources provides an opportunity to investigate mathematics through investigations that span multiple cultures. In particular, three investigations are based on masks from cultures around the world; four investigations are based on a study of country flags; and four investigations are based on games from around the world. The investigations span the range of the five content foci recommended in the *Principles and Standards for School Mathematics* of the National Council of Teachers of Mathematics.

The majority of the investigations can be completed independent of each other, so students can work on only one or two investigations from a particular Internet resource. Some of the investigations are easily completed in a single class period; others are more appropriate for a longer, outside-class project. Teachers may consider different ways to use these investigations depending on the access to computer technology available for their students. The matrix, Investigations by Content and Culture, on pages xii–xiii, cross-references all the investigations by content themes; the table that follows contains only the investigations for the Internet resources. All the investigations are provided on the accompanying CD-ROM.

Reference

National Council of Teachers of Mathematics. 2000. *Principles and Standards for School Mathematics.* Reston, VA: National Council of Teachers of Mathematics.

Internet Investigations by Content and Culture

Resource	Number & Operations	Algebraic Thinking	Geometry	Measurement	Data Analysis & Probability
Masks of the World			• Same difference • Sym . . . Sym . . . Symmetry	• Cover Your Mask	
Flags of the World	• Watch Out for "Red Flags" • Flags of "Golden" Proportions		• Flag Facts • Colorful Percentages	• Colorful Percentages	• Watch Out for "Red Flags"
Games from Around the World	• Get Your Game On		• Hopping on a Scotch • Making a Soccer Ball		• Hopping on a Scotch • Soccer Gone Global

Masks of the World

About the Resource

Cultural Index			Mathematics Index	
Amenable	**B**eneficial	**C**ompelling	Explicit	Implicit
		✓	✓	

This media resource is one that can be used to highlight multiple cultures. The website www.masksoftheworld.com features a collection of tribal masks from numerous countries and regions around the world. For each mask in the collection, a description is provided, including the cultural origin of the mask, its size, and construction material. Although a comparable book resource exists, titled *Masks from Around the World: The Collection of Robert A. Ibold* (Lancaster Museum of Art 2002), the Internet site may be preferred for its accessibility. Groups of students can examine a mask online in detail or compare several masks at one time. In either case, the resource allows students to take their own ethnographic journey to different cultures around the world.

Cultural Group: Multicultural

Mathematical Focus

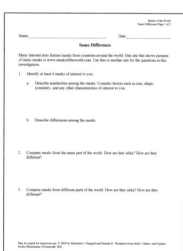

 Investigation: Same Difference

- finding similarities and differences
- spatial sense
- making comparisons using geometric properties

 Investigation: Sym . . . Sym . . . Symmetry

- reflection symmetry
- problem solving

Investigation: Cover Your Mask

- finding area and perimeter
- problem solving

Commentary About the Investigations

In the investigations Same Difference and Sym . . . Sym . . . Symmetry, we suggest using the website www.masksoftheworld.com, although students could use any Internet site with multiple images of masks. These two investigations are independent of each other; however, in Cover Your Mask, students will need to refer to their response to a question in Sym . . . Sym . . . Symmetry.

Same Difference

This investigation introduces students to an Internet site with multiple images of masks. In these tasks, students compare geometric properties of masks in several ways, examining similarities and differences among several masks (Question 1) and comparing masks from the same and different parts of the world (Questions 2 and 3). As students make these comparisons, they should begin to consider common features of masks regardless of origin as well as features that may be unique to a particular region. In contrast, in Question 4 students focus their attention on one mask and describe it in terms of its size, shape, symmetry, and so on.

Students have considerable latitude writing their descriptions but should be encouraged to use geometric properties, such as size or symmetry, as well as appropriate vocabulary. Having students write these descriptions promotes communication in mathematics. Each question is open-ended so that students, whether individually or in groups, can construct extended responses.

Sym . . . Sym . . . Symmetry

Because many tribal masks inherently contain symmetrical features, it is reasonable to have students examine reflection (line) symmetry that appears in different masks. Students may find that different cultures display symmetry in different styles. After students identify a number of masks from different parts of the world, they examine lines of symmetry in a collection of masks they select (Questions 1a and 1b). In Questions 1c and 1d, students connect mathematics properties to the aesthetics of design, specifically considering reasons why one might want a mask with or without lines of symmetry. Students are able to think deeply about the importance of symmetry in Question 2 as they design and decorate their own masks and determine how, or if, the masks reveal line symmetry.

Cover Your Mask

Depending on the Internet site used, the description of each mask may indicate a size or dimension that provides the height of the mask (from top to bottom). Students might use the height dimension and the picture of a tribal mask to estimate a dimension of the width of the mask (from left to right). Using the dimensions, students can then find the perimeter and area of their mask. Depending on students' prior experiences, they might overlay a transparent grid onto an image of the mask so that area can be estimated by counting squares on the grid. A piece of string can be used to estimate the perimeter by tracing the string around the edge of the mask and then measuring the length of the string.

Students are likely to enjoy trying to find the area and perimeter of their own face. They engage in problem solving as they decide on the approaches used to determine these measurements. Students must explain their solution approaches, providing extended explanations as necessary.

References

www.masksoftheworld.com

Lancaster Museum of Art. 2002. *Masks from Around the World: The Collection of Robert A. Ibold.* Lancaster, PA: Lancaster Museum of Art.

CHAPTER 32

Flags of the World

About the Resource

Flags of the World, a media resource located at www.flags.net/fullindex.htm, is one of countless Internet resources that allow the viewer to study flags in detail—a discipline identified as *vexillology*. The

Cultural Index			Mathematics Index	
Amenable	Beneficial	Compelling	Explicit	Implicit
		✓	✓	

site contains vibrant pictures of official flags for over three hundred countries and territories from around the world; each entry also contains basic information about the region represented by the flag. This media resource is inherently multicultural.

Other informative websites for flags include the following:

- http://flagspot.net/flags, which contains answers to frequently asked questions about flags

- http://flagresearchcenter.com/index.html, which discusses vexillology, that is, the academic study of flags

- http://www.enchantedlearning.com/geography/flags/

Cultural Group: Multicultural

Mathematical Focus

 Investigation: Watch Out for "Red Flags"

- collecting data and making observations
- finding percents

 Investigation: Flags of "Golden" Proportions

- determining ratios, including the golden ratio

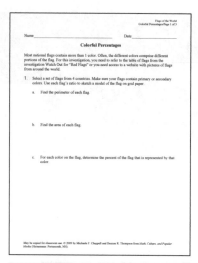

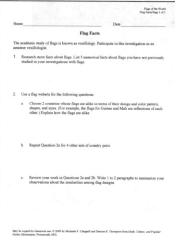

Investigation: Colorful Percentages

- finding percent one figure is of another
- determining perimeter and area measurements
- perimeter and area relationships among similar shapes

Investigation: Flag Facts

- geometric relationships
- making comparisons among figures

Commentary About the Investigations

These four investigations should be considered as a unit. Students need to complete Watch Out for "Red Flags" before completing any other investigations because basic data about flags are collected in this investigation. The social studies connections with the study of flags makes this series of investigations a good opportunity for mathematics and social studies teachers to work together to engage in interdisciplinary instruction.

Watch Out for "Red Flags"

The data collected in this investigation serve as the basis for two other investigations in this chapter, Flags of "Golden" Proportions and Colorful Percentages. Students need access to the Internet or to some comparable resource (e.g., an almanac) that contains pictures of flags from countries around the world. Some of the countries may be unknown to students, so it would be helpful to have a current globe or world map to locate the countries whose flags are being studied.

Students should be encouraged to work on this investigation in small groups so that the collection of data does not become tedious. For students working in groups of four, each student would only need to research flags for ten countries. Because the data from this investigation are used in two other investigations, teachers should have groups compare results with each other and ensure that all groups have the same final set of data.

It may surprise students (and teachers) to learn that flags can be studied as an academic discipline, and that this discipline has a name, *vexillology*. According to http://flagspot.net/flags/faq2.html#prop, red is the most popular color on flags, with 74% of all national flags containing some shade of this color. White is found on 71% of all flags and blue on 50% of flags. Interestingly, all national flags contain at least one of the colors found on the Olympic flag, a white background with five interconnected rings of colors blue, yellow, black, green, and red (http://en.wikipedia.org/wiki/Olympic_flag#Flag).

Flags of "Golden" Proportions

In this investigation, students explore the shapes of national flags. Although the vast majority of flags are nonsquare rectangles (Question 1), some flags are square (e.g., Switzerland) or have unusual shapes (e.g., Nepal).

Throughout history, individuals have sought to design rectangles that are particularly pleasing to the eye. Rectangles whose length-to-width ratio is $\frac{1+\sqrt{5}}{2}$ are known as golden rectangles; many famous buildings (e.g., the Acropolis) are built using this ratio. In fact, posters of world sites or famous artworks designed according to this ratio can be found on the Web (www.gogeometry.com/wonder_world/golden_rectangle_index.html). None of the 40 flags listed in the table is constructed using the golden ratio; however, several flags have ratios close to being golden (e.g., Finland at $1.\overline{63}$; Poland and Sweden at 1.6).

Colorful Percentages

In this investigation, students examine colors on a flag and the percent of that flag represented by each color. In Question 1, they simply find the dimensions of a flag and the percent of the flag represented by each color when a model of that flag has been constructed. Students should be encouraged to work on this activity in small groups, comparing the results for flags from different countries.

In Questions 2 and 3, students explore area and perimeter when flags undergo a given size change. Students should realize that the resulting flags are similar to each other. Although the actual sizes change, the ratio of width to length and the percent represented by each color remain constant. However, the actual area of the entire flag and the area of each color change, as one would expect because more material is needed to make the flag when the flag increases in size. For similar figures with a size change of factor k, the perimeters of the figures compare by a factor of k; the areas of the figures compare by a factor of k^2.

Flag Facts

This investigation is a culminating investigation for this unit on the study of flags. Students have an opportunity to explore some facts about flags that have not previously been studied or to study the same facts previously studied but about new flags. Throughout their completion of the other investigations in this chapter, students have likely noticed similarities among many flags; in fact, some flags seem to be identical to each other under a reflection. So, in this investigation, students are encouraged to find pairs of flags with some similarity of interest and then write a brief report about their observations.

Reference

www.flags.net/fullindex.htm

CHAPTER 33

Games from Around the World

About the Resource

This collection of Internet media resources draws attention to games, mostly traditional in nature, that are played by youngsters and adults around the world. The collection includes the following websites:

Cultural Index			Mathematics Index	
Amenable	**B**eneficial	**C**ompelling	**E**xplicit	**I**mplicit
		✓		✓

- www.topics-mag.com/edition11/games-section.htm
- http://library.thinkquest.org/J0110166/index.html
- www.gameskidsplay.net
- www.soccerballworld.com
- www.soccerhall.org
- www.womensprosoccer.com

The collection of websites features historical details of the featured games, variations of a specific game, or statistical data related to varied aspects of a sport. Because numerous countries have played soccer for many years, soccer is highlighted in this assortment of games as are other games that are familiar to young adolescents.

Cultural Group: Multicultural

Mathematical Focus

Investigation: Hopping on a Scotch

- finding similarities and differences between patterns
- collecting and analyzing data, including box-and-whisker plots
- problem solving with geometric designs

Investigation: Get Your Game On

- interpreting and giving directions
- problem solving

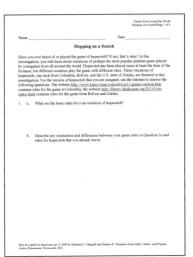

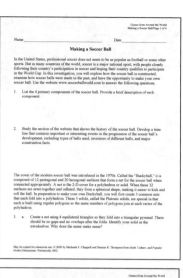

Name_____ Date_____

Making a Soccer Ball

In the United States, professional soccer does not seem to be as popular as football or some other sports. But in many countries of the world, soccer is a major national sport, with people closely following their country's participation in soccer and hoping their country qualifies to participate in the World Cup. In this investigation, you will explore how the soccer ball is constructed, examine how soccer balls were made in the past, and have the opportunity to make your own soccer ball. Use the website www.soccerballworld.com to answer the following questions.

1. List the 4 primary components of the soccer ball. Provide a brief description of each component.

2. Study the section of the website that shows the history of the soccer ball. Develop a time line that contains important or interesting events in the progression of the soccer ball's development, including types of balls used, inventors of different balls, and major construction facts.

The cover of the modern soccer ball was introduced in the 1970s. Called the "Buckyball," it is composed of 12 pentagonal and 20 hexagonal surfaces that form a net for the soccer ball when connected appropriately. A *net* is the 2-D cover for a polyhedron or solid. When these 32 surfaces are sewn together and inflated, they form a spherical shape, making it easier to kick and roll the ball. In preparation to make your own Buckyball, you will first create 5 common nets that each fold into a polyhedron. These 5 solids, called the Platonic solids, are special in that each is built using regular polygons so the same numbers of polygons join at each vertex of the polyhedron.

3. a. Create a net using 4 equilateral triangles so they fold into a triangular pyramid. There should be no gaps and no overlaps after the folds. Identify your solid as the *tetrahedron*. Why does the name make sense?

May be copied for classroom use. © 2009 by Michaela F. Chappell and Denisse R. Thompson from *Math, Culture, and Popular Media* (Heinemann: Portsmouth, NH).

Name_____ Date_____

Soccer Gone Global

Soccer is a game played around the world by both boys and girls. Sometimes, young children play soccer on coed teams, as children get older, they often play on all male or all female teams. Soccer is a bigger sport in the rest of the world than in the United States. In fact, much of the world becomes engrossed with soccer during the period of time when the World Cup is being contested.

How do men and women compare in their soccer statistics?

1. Visit the website http://national.soccerhall.org/US_NationalTeamRec_Intro.htm to find statistics about the U.S. men's and women's national soccer teams. These are the teams that compete for the United States in soccer competitions with other countries.

   a. Under the heading U.S. Men's National Team History & Information, click on the link for "All-Time Leaders." There are tables showing the top 10 players for caps, goals, assists, and points. For the top 10 goal scorers, analyze the data for the number of goals, including the mean and median number of goals and the range.

   b. Repeat Question 1a for the number of points scored by the top 10 male players.

2. Return to the page http://national.soccerhall.org/US_NationalTeamRec_Intro.htm. Now find the section containing statistics about the U.S. Women's National Team & History. Click on the link for "All-Time Leaders."

   a. Repeat the analysis in Question 1a for the number of goals for the top women players.

May be copied for classroom use. © 2009 by Michaela F. Chappell and Denisse R. Thompson from *Math, Culture, and Popular Media* (Heinemann: Portsmouth, NH).

Investigation: Making a Soccer Ball

- identifying geometric solids, including their faces, vertices, and edges
- building nets for solids

Investigation: Soccer Gone Global

- collecting data
- data analysis, including mean, median, and graphical displays
- statistical reasoning and interpretation

Commentary About the Investigations

These four investigations can be completed independent of each other. Students need access to the Internet for all four investigations. For Making a Soccer Ball, students need access to polydrons (i.e., a manipulative consisting of polygon pieces that snap together) or to cutouts of equilateral triangles, regular pentagons, and regular hexagons.

Hopping on a Scotch

This investigation calls attention to the game of hopscotch, perhaps one of the oldest known games that youngsters have played around the world. Although the game is familiar, students may be surprised that variations of the game exist in different countries.

Students will first need to conduct some brief Internet research to explore their group's variation of the hopscotch game (Question 1); although we have provided only three variations, teachers could include other variations if desired. Using the indicated websites, students should be able to note the rules for playing the game and then compare those rules to more familiar hopscotch rules from their own childhood.

Question 2 provides another opportunity for students to compare and contrast hopscotch patterns. Most students should be able to find the area of their pattern relatively easily given the indicated information (Question 2c). However, those individuals with the Bolivian pattern may need help with the formula for the area of a semicircle depending on their prior experiences with area formulas for this shape.

In Question 3, students design a 100-foot-long hopscotch court that meets a given number of conditions. This is an open task and there is considerable room for students to use their own creativity in the solution. Students should be expected to choose reasonable sizes for their shapes so that a player could easily hop from one shape to another. Likewise, they should be cognizant of the number of hops that someone could make on a single foot before needing to place both feet on the ground for a rest.

For Question 4, students actually play hopscotch in small groups on different patterns. Perhaps mathematics teachers could coordinate with physical education teachers so students collect the data in PE class and then analyze it during mathematics class. Once the groups have collected the data on number of hops each member makes, the class can examine the data using box plots. Students could compare results for the different variations provided in the investigation. Alternatively, students could collect data for the hopscotch patterns they created in Question 3.

Get Your Game On

This investigation involves students in learning about traditional games that are played by youngsters from around the world. Eight traditional games are listed from different countries in Africa, Asia, North America, and South America. The investigation is designed for students to work in groups to explore a game, including its origin, rules of play, and any mathematics that is potentially applied in the play of the game. After groups gather and record this information, they are to play the game as a group and then teach other class members to play the game. Ideally, if groups of three to four students research just one game, the entire class will "get their game on" for eight different games as played by youngsters from around the world.

Students may be familiar with a particular game, but they may not be familiar with the variation of it as practiced by the country indicated in the table. So, they should be encouraged to conduct the game according to the given rules and to avoid tweaking the game to fit how they are familiar with it. As for the description of potential mathematics embedded in the game, students may need some initial examples to help them generate additional ideas for the mathematics within their game. Nevertheless, they should be held accountable for thinking about the math ideas that could be applied to their game; ideas can range from simple number ideas to geometry or measurement ideas. For instance, in Ampé (from Ghana), students might study patterns to record which foot the leader thrusts into the center of the circle; after a certain time, students might predict which foot is more likely to be used on a given round.

Teachers are not limited to this list of international games but could make replacements as desired. For instance, the games listed are quite fitting for younger middle-grades students. Hence, for older students, teachers might select a set of international games more appropriate to their students' age or grade range. However, teachers should keep in mind that even older students might be interested in playing some childhood games that they may or may not have played while growing up.

Making a Soccer Ball

In this investigation, students explore how soccer balls are constructed, examine how they were made in the past, and create a model of a soccer ball. The investigation starts by having students describe the 4 primary components of a soccer ball (Question 1) before they develop a time line (Question 2) of important years and events in the history of the development of the ball. Different time lines can be developed depending on those events that students find the most interesting in the history of the ball's development.

In Question 3, students progress through a series of questions that introduce the concept of nets. Students may have had previous experience working with 2-D nets for 3-D solids; however, in this question students focus only on nets for special polyhedra, namely the Platonic solids. These solids can be made using multiple copies of cardstock cutouts of equilateral triangles, squares, and regular pentagons (e.g., cutouts using an Ellison machine); if teachers need to construct their own templates, they need to ensure that there is a consistent length for the edge of the 3 shapes so that they fit together. If available, teachers may have students use a commercial manipulative that allows students to build solids by hand (e.g., polydrons). Teachers may want to have pictures of the Platonic solids available for students to have a visual model of what they should expect; the website http://mathworld.wolfram.com/PlatonicSolid.html contains a picture of each solid as well as the required net.

Once students have made the Platonic solids, then they should record the information requested in Question 4. Organizing this info will help students see patterns in the numbers of faces, vertices, and edges, leading ultimately to the famous pattern for Euler's formula: $F + V - 2 = E$. In Question 5, students have an opportunity to make a model of the soccer ball (the famous "Buckyball"). Again, students could use polydrons or cardstock cutouts of 12 regular pentagonal and 20 regular hexagonal shapes. Regardless, students will need to conduct this task in small groups so they can cooperate and work together as a team to tape or snap all 32 faces together. Figure 33.1 illustrates our version of the Buckyball made with polydrons.

We suggest that teachers allow ample time for this portion of the task; although students will likely find the making of the soccer ball engaging and illuminating, they will need time to join the faces for the nets and determine the best way to fold the faces into the soccer ball. Last, students return to the table in Question 4 to determine the number of faces, edges, and vertices for their soccer ball and verify that earlier patterns observed in the table also apply to the truncated icosahedron. For further information about creating a truncated icosahedron, see http://en.wikipedia.org/wiki/Truncated_icosahedron.

FIGURE 33.1
Buckyball Made with Polydrons

Soccer Gone Global

This investigation provides an opportunity for students to investigate statistics related to soccer. Although soccer is not a big sport professionally in the United States, it is a major sport in many other countries around the world. Fans often become obsessed with their local soccer club (e.g., think about the English or Spanish professional soccer clubs and their fans); entire nations become glued to the television to watch the games during World Cup competitions.

In the United States, the women's national soccer team has often performed better than the men's national team. Questions 1–4 encourage students to draw comparisons between statistics for top male and female players from the national teams. In addition to determining basic statistics, students should be encouraged to graph the data using a box-and-whisker plot. Such a display illustrates the spread of the data and can accommodate differences in the sizes of the sample, 10 for men and 5 for women as of the end of 2008.

Question 5 focuses on the inauguration of women's professional soccer slated to begin play in 2009. Determining the number of games to be played if every team plays every other team just once is a variation of the classic handshake problem. To determine the number of games, imagine each team as the vertex of a polygon. The number of games to be played among n teams is the number of diagonals in an n-gon together with the number of edges, which is given by the formula $\frac{n(n-1)}{2}$.

Students may be surprised at the size of many stadiums throughout the United States and the world, the focus of Question 6. The given website includes not only the name and size of the stadium but the sport that is played there, using an icon to illustrate the sport (or to indicate that the stadium is multiuse). When students draw comparisons for stadiums in different regions of the world, they should be encouraged to support their comparisons with actual data analysis (e.g., mean, median, range) and possible graphical displays (e.g., box-and-whisker plots).

References

www.topics-mag.com/edition11/games-section.htm

http://library.thinkquest.org/J0110166/index.html

www.gameskidsplay.net

www.soccerballworld.com

http://national.soccerhall.org/US_NationalTeamRec_Intro.htm

www.womensprosoccer.com

http://worldstadiums.com

Novel Approaches to Weave Culture and Mathematics Through Media

As we conducted research for this book and collected resources to write the investigations, it became clear that many of the culturally based media resources connect in intriguing ways across cultures and across disciplines. These connections provide teachers additional instructional approaches during use of these resources. Therefore, we conclude this volume with three chapters, each of which presents a novel approach that emerged during the development phase; these chapters also contain more examples of culturally based media resources. These chapters illustrate, respectively, how one resource can address different content disciplines, how numerous resources from many cultures can accentuate one thematic topic, and how one resource can address many cultures simultaneously.

CHAPTER 34

One Resource . . . Many Disciplines

D ue to limited instructional time as well as structured schedules in many middle schools, teachers are often interested in using mathematics tasks that engage students with multiple content topics simultaneously. Such tasks have students approach content from multiple perspectives, which can help them develop a robust understanding of the subject. In addition, tasks that deal with multiple content topics enable teachers to address more content during a class period and provide opportunities for students to make important connections. For instance, the investigation Whales and More Whales from the film *Spirit of the Animals* (Chapter 7) includes work with number computations related to percent change, measurement, and data analysis through graphical displays. Likewise, the investigation Fashionable Fashions from the film *Selena* (Chapter 9) incorporates algebraic expressions with geometric designs.

Just as a media resource can help teachers develop instruction that addresses multiple mathematics content topics, one media resource can often serve as a basis for instruction across different disciplines. Many middle school teams have times throughout the year in which the teams attempt to engage in interdisciplinary thematic instruction; teachers often raise concerns about how to include mathematics in such interdisciplinary instruction. Resources, such as those in this volume, provide a basis for interdisciplinary instruction with a cultural perspective that includes mathematics as well as other subject areas. We believe instruction that weaves culture and mathematics can be integrated throughout the school year and not reserved for inclusion only at special times. Moreover, the potential for these media resources to facilitate the inclusion of mathematics into thematic interdisciplinary units should not be overlooked.

The discussion that follows highlights three exemplars from three different cultural perspectives that illustrate how this interdisciplinary approach can work in middle school. Two exemplars are based on films and one on a book.

Exemplar Resource—African American Video: *A Raisin in the Sun*

Originally a play written by Lorraine Hansberry, this classic film portrays an African American family, including the matriarch mother, her daughter, and her son with his wife and eleven-year-old boy; the family lives together in a small two-bedroom high-rise in a depressed area on the south side of Chicago. In the aftermath of the death of the matriarch's husband, the family is expecting a $10,000 life insurance check. The plot revolves around conflicts that arise among family members regarding how to use the money once it arrives. Mother wants to use a portion to buy the family a modest home and save for her daughter's medical school tuition; Walter Lee, her son, wants to invest the money in a liquor store business deal.

Cultural Index			Mathematics Index	
Amenable	Beneficial	Compelling	Explicit	Implicit
	✓		✓	

Cultural Group: African and African American

Length: 128 minutes

Rating: Not rated (According to Wikipedia, the 1961 film was designated in 2005 for preservation in the National Film Registry in the Library of Congress because of its cultural significance.)

In 2008, a made-for-television production recreated the film. Although the recreation is true to the original in most respects, the recreation gives a bit more prominence to Walter Lee's alcohol use and to his wife's possible decision to have an abortion. So, we prefer to use the 1961 version with students; this is the version on which the remainder of this discussion and classroom results are based.

Mathematical Focus

Investigation: Math Survey *(reprinted on CD-ROM with permission from the National Council of Teachers of Mathematics)*

Investigation: Housing Prices and Costs *(reprinted on CD-ROM with permission from the National Council of Teachers of Mathematics)*

- data analysis and statistics
- creating box-and-whisker plots
- problem solving

Investigation: All in a Day's Work *(reprinted on CD-ROM with permission from the National Council of Teachers of Mathematics)*

- generating values in a table and generalizing patterns
- graphing coordinate pairs from a linear equation
- problem solving

Commentary About the Investigations

We first described these investigations in Chappell and Thompson (2000a), including information about how students in two eighth-grade mathematics classes engaged with the activities based on the film. Together with the students, we watched the film in the mathematics class in early spring. Afterward, students completed the Math Survey (see the CD-ROM) to share their views about the film and about topics they would be interested in studying. Unbeknownst to us at the time, students had recently read the play and acted out the parts in their English class; thus, they were amused to view a film related to what they had just read. The students were familiar with the film's plot and the issues the film raises from their encounters with it in their English class. The use of the play in English class before we used it in mathematics class helped us begin to consider the use of such resources as a basis for interdisciplinary instruction.

Using a Math Survey related to the film and then discussing the results with students enable teachers to gauge how students analyzed the film and interpreted different social issues surrounding it. Expanding this discussion across different subject areas presents opportunities for teachers to maximize use of the film, making natural interdisciplinary links during instruction. In the next section, we examine some possibilities for using this one resource across several disciplines other than mathematics.

The Discipline of . . .

- *English*—After the family has decided to buy and move into a home in an upscale area of Chicago, they receive a visit from a lawyer representing the homeowner's association of the new neighborhood. He offers them a refund of their $3,500 down payment and a bonus if they relinquish their purchase of the home in the neighborhood. From a literature perspective, students could read the play, watch the classic film, and study the plot, setting, and characters. Students from all ethnic backgrounds could write essays on how they have felt when faced with unwelcome or uncomfortable situations, including situations in which prejudice is clearly evident.

- *Social Studies*—At another point in the film, Walter Lee and his mother are in a heated confrontation about what constitutes life. He exclaims that it is *money*; his mother retorts that it is *freedom*. Students could engage in discussions and exercises that reveal what the comments mean based on the social and political climate of the time.

A Raisin in the Sun
All in a Day's Work Page 1 of 2

Name_____ Date_____ Period_____

All in a Day's Work

1. Remember when Walter Lee became distraught about not being able to make the investment that he wanted to make? He skipped work for three days. Estimate his salary as a chauffeur, and compute how much base pay he missed for those three days.

Three individuals have the following salary and raise schedules.

Person A makes $30 000 and expects a raise of $1 000 each year.

Person B makes $30 000 and expects a raise of $2 000 each year.

Person C makes $30 000 and expects a raise of $3 500 each year.

2. Complete the following table showing each person's salary for the indicated years

Year	Person A	Person B	Person C
0	$30 000	$30 000	$30 000
1	$31 000		
2			
3			
4			
5			
6			
x			

- *Business*—Walter Lee had friends in the dry-cleaning business. However, Walter Lee gave $6,500 toward a deal to pay for licensing a liquor store business even though his mother opposed starting such a business; Walter Lee later lost this money because one of the partners swindled him. This setting provides an opportunity for students to study factors essential to starting a new business as an entrepreneur (e.g., starting capital, incorporating expenses). Students could also explore basics of business ethics and legal issues revolving around embezzlement of funds.

- *Actuarial Science*—The entire plot of the film revolves around a $10,000 life insurance check. Students could study values of life insurance policies and the factors that influence premiums paid on such policies. Although students tend not to study actuarial science in schools, they do begin studying underlying concepts that link to topics in actuarial science. Increasingly more schools and districts are incorporating financial literacy into the curriculum, and insurance is often a topic connected to financial mathematics courses.

- *Financial Planning*—The mother wanted to invest a portion of the $10,000 and place some in a checking account. Students could compare interest earned on different banking and investment products, like checking and savings accounts, mutual funds, or certificates of deposit.

All of the possibilities discussed for different disciplines are extracted from various scenes in *A Raisin in the Sun*; teachers can explore them to the depth they feel is appropriate for their students. Although not all middle schools will include every discipline mentioned previously, the specific ideas can appear in different subject areas. The suggestions provided are just some of the options that exist for teachers, or teams of teachers, who desire to offer different choices in their curriculum for their students.

Exemplar Resource—Asian Literature Book: *A Grain of Rice*

A popular Asian folktale, this book reveals how a peasant farmer uses his cleverness to become a wealthy man. Initially, the farmer makes repeated requests to the emperor to marry his daughter but is refused each time. One day, the princess becomes ill and the farmer prepares a potion that cures her. When pressed to think of a reward other than to marry the princess, the farmer requests a single grain of rice, with the grains doubling each day for the next one hundred days. The emperor agrees to the request and has the rice carried to the farmer each day in elaborate containers; after forty days, the emperor realizes that the country will soon run out of rice and be bankrupt. Permission is then granted for the farmer to marry the emperor's daughter and the farmer's reward in rice is suspended.

Cultural Index			Mathematics Index	
Amenable	Beneficial	Compelling	Explicit	Implicit
		✓	✓	

Cultural Group: Asian and Pacific Islanders

Mathematical Focus

Investigation: The Peasant Problem Solver (*reprinted on CD-ROM by permission of the National Council of Teachers of Mathematics*)

- algebraic thinking
- scientific notation
- exploring exponential patterns
- graphing exponential relationships
- problem solving

Investigation: Storing a Fortune (*reprinted on CD-ROM by permission of the National Council of Teachers of Mathematics*)

- estimating volume measurement
- problem solving

Investigation: Preparing a Feast (*reprinted on CD-ROM by permission of the National Council of Teachers of Mathematics*)

- problem solving
- number operations
- statistics

Commentary About the Investigations

Detailed discussion of these investigations can be found in "Exploring Mathematics Through Asian Folktales" (Thompson, Chappell, and Austin 1999). This print literature resource is one of several Asian folktales that blend mathematical patterns within the story plot. Teachers across several disciplines can implement this version of the story or similar versions to provide middle-grades students with interdisciplinary activities. Possibilities for using this resource in disciplines other than mathematics might look like the following.

The Discipline of . . .

- *English*—Students could simply read this book and other versions of the folktale as part of reading literature in the classroom. As we have stated earlier, "Every child likes a good story!" In particular, middle-grades students would appreciate the peasant farmer having "gotten one over" on the emperor. They could also write essays about how to overcome odds through perseverance and cleverness and through problem solving.

- *Social Studies*—Students could examine the role that rice plays as a staple in people's diet in certain regions of the world, including geographic connections to climate and rice production. They could also explore social, political, and financial implications for countries to keep large amounts of rice stored for uncertain times.

- *Business*—Students could debate and discuss the business strategy of the peasant farmer to gain not only the rice but also the princess as his bride. They could examine the global impact of the rice industry and the extent to which rice has contributed to the economy of different countries.

- *Science*—Students might investigate characteristics of different types of rice, including growing conditions, cooking conditions, nutrition, natural pests, and so on.

- *Character*—Because many schools include some aspects of character education, students could discuss character implications in the story. Traits like perseverance, honor, cleverness, and knowledge of mathematics enable the hero of the folktale to achieve his goal. Students can explore how these traits helped the farmer achieve success.

Exemplar Resource—Native American and Indigenous Peoples Film: *Rabbit-Proof Fence*

Investigations related to this film resource are discussed in Chapter 8 and are not repeated here. However, recall that the film is based on a true story, which adds another dimension to the scope of its use in a classroom context. People often display an entirely different set of emotions when they know a film is based on or inspired by true events. This resource can offer much in the way of an interdisciplinary focus. We offer and elaborate on a few suggestions that teachers might consider as they use the resource across several subject areas in middle school.

The Discipline of . . .

- *English*—There are many poignant scenes in this film, any of which could serve as the basis for students to write brief essays or reports about their response to the scenes. For example, students could record how they think the girls—Molly, Daisy, and Gracie—might have felt when "stolen" from their homes. Students could also create their own literature stories about situations in their own lives, and share them with the class if willing to do so.

- *Social Studies*—Based on the maps and clues from the film, students could sketch the track of the girls from the settlement back to their home in Jigalong. Then they could compare that sketch to a current-day map of the continent and note the position of the rabbit-proof fences. Older middle-grades students might discuss the racial implications related to Australia's policy to take Aborigines children from their homes to be raised as another race of people; indeed, there are current-day implications for these "stolen generations." Students could compare the situation in Australia to similar situations in the United States in terms of slavery or the removal of Native American children from their parents to be raised in boarding schools as white children.

- *Science*—Students could explore environmental issues related to animals and their natural predators, including potential environmental disasters when the balance related to the two is disturbed. Connected to this, students could explore why rabbits were such a problem that fences were needed. In addition, they could investigate particular diseases that might occur when animal pests have close encounters with food crops.

- *Business*—Students might investigate any potential financial benefits for the Australian government that resulted from this policy. The "stolen" children were raised to become domestic workers. So, students could explore how this policy might have been profitable for those who were running the settlement.

Summary

The three exemplars discussed in this chapter are ideal resources for use across subject areas taught in middle-grades classrooms. Films and books reflect the culture of the people represented in the resource, making media resources powerful tools to use in middle-grades instruction. "Approaching the media in an interdisciplinary format as suggested here promotes collaboration among teachers of different subjects; it also allows one to obtain the maximum benefit from the use of the media [resource]" (Chappell and Thompson 2000b, 142).

References

Print References

Chappell, Michaele, and Denisse R. Thompson. 2000a. "*A Raisin in the Sun*: Fostering Cultural Connections with a Classic Movie." *Mathematics Teaching in the Middle School* 6 (4): 222–25 and 233–35.

Chappell, Michaele F., and Denisse R. Thompson. 2000b. "Fostering Multicultural Connections in Mathematics through Media." In *Changing the Faces of Mathematics: Perspectives on African Americans,* edited by M. Strutchens, M. Johnson, and W. Tate, 135–50. Reston, VA: National Council of Teachers of Mathematics.

Thompson, Denisse R., Michaele F. Chappell, and Richard A. Austin. 1999. "Exploring Mathematics through Asian Folktales." In *Changing the Faces of Mathematics: Perspectives on Asian American and Pacific Islanders,* edited by W. G. Secada and C. A. Edwards, 1–11. Reston, VA: National Council of Teachers of Mathematics.

Media References

A Raisin in the Sun. 1961. Produced by David Susskind and Philip Rose. Directed by Daniel Petric. Written by Lorraine Hansberry. 128 minutes. Columbia Pictures. Videocassette.

A Raisin in the Sun. 2008. Produced by John M. Eckert. Directed by Kenny Leon. 131 minutes. Sony Pictures Television. Film.

Pittman, Helena Clare. 1986. *A Grain of Rice.* New York: Bantam Skylark.

CHAPTER 35

One Theme . . . Many Resources and Many Cultures

As mentioned in Chapter 34, it is common for middle schools to organize their curriculum around interdisciplinary units that focus on a specific topic or theme at least once during the school year. Culturally based media resources can serve as the basis for such units by offering students different perspectives on the thematic topic while enabling them to access the content ideas embedded within the unit. So, in this chapter, we briefly examine one thematic topic that is evident in several resources featured in this volume. The discussion reveals how several resources that highlight different cultures can still facilitate study of a single topic—in this case, young entrepreneurs.

Exemplar Theme—Becoming an Entrepreneur

Teachers might question whether *becoming an entrepreneur* is an appropriate topic for middle-grades students given that adolescents in fifth through eighth grades are often too young to work in a business environment. However, students at these levels often baby-sit or mow lawns, so they really are young entrepreneurs. In addition, adolescents are often participants on popular television shows, such as *American Idol* or *America's Got Talent*, indicating desires to establish a professional career early.

More than ever before, teens and adolescents worldwide are generating witty inventions, day-trading stocks, selling items on eBay, and dealing in real estate. An Internet search on topics such as teen entrepreneurs, teen millionaires, kids and money, or children and finances yields numerous websites and products around this topic. Thus, becoming an entrepreneur is a theme that middle-grades students are likely to find interesting and engaging, particularly as they study it with different culturally based resources.

The resources we discuss in the following sections illustrate how characters from different cultures deal with situations surrounding entrepreneurship. Students can consider similarities and differences among the entrepreneurs and consider traits that contribute to their success or nonsuccess. To examine *becoming an entrepreneur*, we revisit a sampling of culturally based resources from earlier chapters in this volume and illustrate how each conveys a strong message regarding this topic.

Many Resources and Many Cultures . . .

- *African American Film Resource: The Pursuit of Happyness*—Discussed in Chapter 5, this film resource is based on the true story of Chris Gardner, who became a salesman for a brokerage firm and worked on Wall Street; he eventually started his own securities company. (The film takes a bit of cinematic license with the story. In the film, Chris sells bone density scanners, but he apparently did not sell such products in real life.) Chris seemed to be a successful seller, whether selling investment products or selling himself. He was driven by the pursuit to be happy based on his perception of success. Aside from engaging in the set of investigations related to the film (Getting Rid of the Machines, Making Cold Calls, Numbers in Your Head, and Solving the Rubik's Cube), students could study Chris' entrepreneurial skills as well as personality traits that made him successful. For instance, Chris exhibited determination to sell each of the bone density scanners on which he had spent his life savings. Likewise, while in the brokerage training program, he was creative in developing strategies that saved time and permitted him to make more cold calls to solicit potential clients. What lessons might students take from the film that would help them become successful entrepreneurs?

- *Native American Film Resource: The Lost Child*—This film resource is discussed in Chapter 6. While students undertake the set of investigations for the film (Weaving on the Loom, Dyeing Wool, and Rug Design), they may recall that the mother of Odett Marie (the major character) had supported her family by weaving and selling her wares. This is one reason Odett Marie wanted to learn the weaving process. As a weaver, her mother would have demonstrated basic entrepreneurial skills by creating her own products—likely rugs and quilts— and then selling them at the market for profit. Students might investigate how supply and demand are interrelated to determine prices for goods and the potential profit available to the entrepreneur.

- *Hispanic Film Resource: Selena*—Chapter 9 contains the discussion for this film resource as well as the set of investigations (Are You in My Space?, Start Up That Band!, and Fashionable Fashions). Based on true events in Selena's young life, the overall story line of the film undoubtedly illustrates the entrepreneurial capabilities of her entire family. Because he had a background with bands and music gigs, Selena's dad was instrumental in starting her band by purchasing the necessary instruments for his children. Thus, the personality trait of initiative was present in the Dad as well as in the other family members, such as the first time Selena performed using a bustier. At one point in the film, the family owned and operated a restaurant where the young band played and provided entertainment; when the restaurant went out of business, the family used the situation to their advantage to begin traveling to perform. Eventually, the family enterprise grew into a major operation; as

Selena and the band became more popular, the family traveled from city to city and into neighboring Mexico to conduct concerts. In addition, Selena created the attire for herself and her band members, ultimately opening her own fashion boutique to sell designs she created. Many entrepreneurial traits are demonstrated in this film, including responsibility, diligence, creativity, and initiative; the failure of the restaurant suggests that when one door closes, another opportunity often awaits for those willing to seize it.

- *African Book Resource: Beatrice's Goat* (McBrier 2001)—This resource and the related investigations (Goat Figure and Adopt a Goat) are discussed in Chapter 13. Through this resource, students can realize the power of small changes to have major impact. Entrepreneurial endeavors do not have to be large enterprises; in this case, a single goat made available to Beatrice's family had the potential to lift her family from poverty. The resource also highlights the power of individuals to be positive forces for change in the world. Rather than just donating money to provide relief to help individuals in third-world countries, donating an animal provides long-term relief by helping a family become financially independent.

- *African American Book Resource: Vision of Beauty: The Story of Sarah Breedlove Walker* (Lasky 2000)—A summary of this book resource and the investigations (Company Earnings, Products and Profits, and It's All About "Style") are included in Chapter 19. Madame C. J. Walker was what one might call an entrepreneur extraordinaire. She was so resolved to find a solution to the hair problems she encountered that she pioneered the industry for black women's hair and beauty care products, ultimately founding her own manufacturing company. Her company became one of the largest in America during the early 1900s and a financial success, remaining in business for nearly 80 years. Madame Walker was philanthropic, a strong characteristic of great entrepreneurs, and to this day, the legacy of her wealth and philanthropy lives. The story of her life demonstrates many entrepreneurial traits, including being a problem solver, having the courage to stand and face potential opposition, and persevering through hard times. Furthermore, she thought about how to grow her business, cleverly training her agents to conduct sales while, at the same time, signing customers to become new agents. What lessons might students learn from this resource that would help them begin their own business?

Summary

From the media resources discussed in this chapter, it is evident that rich and bountiful examples across many ethnic and cultural groups illustrate the power of entrepreneurial activities to influence the lives of people. With a little research, teachers can locate varied cultural resources for many other thematic topics. Through such resources, not only can students learn mathematics, but they can learn about the world in which they live and develop practical skills for life.

References

Lasky, Kathryn. 2000. *Vision of Beauty: The Story of Sarah Breedlove Walker.* Cambridge: Candlewick.

McBrier, Page. 2001. *Beatrice's Goat.* New York: Atheneum.

Selena. 1997. Produced by Moctesuma Esparza. Written and Directed by Gregory Nava. 128 minutes. Warner Brothers. Film.

The Lost Child. 2000. Produced by Richard Welsh. Directed by Karen Arthur and Teleplay by Sally Beth Robinson. 98 minutes. Hallmark Hall of Fame Productions. Film.

The Pursuit of Happyness. 2006. Produced by Todd Black, Jason Blumenthal, Steve Tisch, James Lassiter, and Will Smith. Directed by Gabriele Muccino. 117 minutes. Columbia Pictures. Film.

CHAPTER 36

One Resource . . . Many Cultures

Many media resources reflect multiple cultures concomitantly. Clearly, this is a benefit to middle school teachers who often have students of diverse cultural backgrounds in their classrooms. Because U.S. public schools tend to reflect patterns of diversity similar to those of their surrounding neighborhoods and communities, today's classrooms often have students whose mother tongue is not English, likely signaling the presence of a range of cultural groups present in the classroom. Thus, it becomes all the more important for teachers to create a culturally relevant classroom environment.

Resources that reflect multiple cultures can motivate a range of students, drawing them into learning mathematics. Such resources can help students identify with their own culture as well as with the cultures of their peers. When teachers implement such media resources into instruction, then in a real sense they promote a culturally relevant classroom (Ladson-Billings 1995).

In the following sections, we highlight four resources that enable teachers to address multiple cultures simultaneously. One resource is the Olympics, a major sporting competition that brings together athletes from around the world. Two resources, masks and flags, are representative of many cultures and are widely available via the Internet. Biographies, the fourth resource, provide opportunities to consider important figures in various cultures and how those figures might have used mathematics formally or informally.

An Exemplar Resource of "Olympic" Proportions

Artwork, photography, board games, or sports are just some of the real-world media resources in which cultural perspectives are represented. Consider a prominent media event recognized as the greatest sports festival and the "most elite sports competition on earth," the Olympic Games (see the resource by Oxlade [2005]). Whether held during the summer or winter, for all athletes or for those with special needs (Special Olympics or the Paralympics), the games include athletes from numerous countries around the world. Some countries, such as the United States, have hundreds of athletes competing; other countries may have just a handful of athletes. This worldwide event captures the imagination of peoples from many cultures around the world, who unite to recognize and celebrate the achievements of those who have sacrificed in an attempt to become world champions in their sport. At each Olympics, new sports are added and others are dropped to reflect the influence of diverse cultures on the overall direction of the Olympics.

Teachers can extract a staggering number of mathematics ideas from Olympics data. In the following paragraphs, we offer a brief sampling of ideas appropriate for middle-grades students who use the Olympics as a resource.

- *Data Collection and Statistics*—The volume of statistical data about the Olympic games is astounding. Comparing data from Olympian personalities within the same sport is one way this bountiful resource can be used to bring a cultural texture to the classroom environment. Although individuals from diverse cultural backgrounds are studied under the microscope, mathematics tasks can pull ideas together and help students make sense of the data detailing their physical achievements. Documentaries are often produced about Olympic legends (e.g., *Wilma* [1977] about track star Wilma Rudolph or *The Jesse Owens Story* [1984] about track legend Jesse Owens), and viewing these films can inspire students as they explore mathematics. In addition, unusual sport circumstances, such as a bobsled team from Jamaica, can serve as the basis for other mathematics explorations (see the film *Cool Runnings* [1993]).

- *Measurement*—Students can investigate distances traveled to the host country/city from the different participating countries, computing measures of central tendency or displaying the data visually. Additionally, students can study particular competitions up close. For instance, the choreography routines of the figure skaters or gymnasts provide opportunities to blend mathematics and physics, which are essential to the routines.

- *Number Sense and Operations*—Millions of people throughout the world watch various parts of the Olympics, from the opening ceremony to the closing celebration. Thousands gather in person to attend different events and competitions. Students can obtain data related to audience attendance and analyze the data.

- *Finances*—Enormous costs are generated for a city to host the Olympics, such as preparation of venues, facilities, manpower, and so on; just competing to be a host city is a major financial undertaking. However, cities like to host the event because they reap financial benefits for many years following the event. Students could study some aspects of the financial implications for a host city.

Two Exemplar Internet Media Resources: Masks and Flags of the World

We review here two examples discussed previously in Chapters 31 and 32 as Internet media resources. Both Masks of the World and Flags of the World inherently feature multicultural elements and, hence, are ideal resources to examine multiple cultures at one time. In the investigations in Masks of the World, students examine similarities and differences among several masks and compare masks from different regions of the world. Additionally, students see that different cultures display varied interpretations and styles of mathematics ideas within their masks, such as line symmetry.

These tasks help teachers accomplish at least one of four approaches Wiest (2001) discusses as appropriate multicultural mathematics instruction—that is, incorporating into the curriculum formal and informal mathematics practices of people of different cultures. Teachers employ this approach when they have students study the masks in detail. The masks are authentic expressions of peoples' styles of thinking about symmetrical relations and applications. Moreover, potential benefits that students gain from the mere exposure to images and descriptions of masks from around the world are incalculable because exposure alone helps students realize they are part of a global world. Such classroom experiences can contribute positively to shape and/or reshape students' views of other cultures. As Wiest comments, students have opportunities to then "see that 'different' does not equate with 'deficient'" (2001, 19).

Revisiting the Flags of the World resource, clearly there is much to learn about nations around the world through the study of their flags. On the surface, students may initially think about country flags from purely an aesthetic perspective, noticing general appearances and colors, emblems, and so on. However, the investigations in Flags of the World require students to examine a wide array of countries, comparing and contrasting their flags' shapes, sizes in terms of area and perimeter, color patterns, and basic designs. Each country's flag assuredly reflects its own historical backdrop as well as the meaning and traditions valued and transmitted by the country through the public display of its banner. When students are studying flags of different countries throughout the world, they are studying the histories, traditions, beliefs, and ideas of those countries—in essence, the cultural milieu making each country distinct from all others.

Faul (1997) developed a book resource in which he told the story of the African continent through a look at its countries' flags. Brief historical comments about the country are provided, including information about independence and the development of the flag after independence. In another example, Jones (2000) describes how she uses flags as physical models to introduce mathematical ideas to inservice teachers and their students. In addition to learning about the flags of forty-four countries comprising sub-Saharan Africa, participants learn about the history and geography of the countries. Mathematically, teachers and students learn or enhance skills in classification by exploring attributes, intersections of sets, data collection and analysis, area measurement, fractions, decimals, and percents. Jones states, "Curricular materials that provide multicultural connections to mathematics simulate the learning of traditional curricular topics and encourage students' success by making mathematics relevant to the world in which they live" (2000, 151).

Biographies: Learning About Important Cultural Figures

Many middle schools incorporate reading across the curriculum. Biographies of important cultural figures often provide opportunities to learn about individuals who have cultural significance. Although a given book will focus on only one individual from one culture, a series of biographies provides an opportunity to consider similarities and differences among individuals from many cultures and their accomplishments.

Certainly, there are biographies of important athletes (e.g., Jesse Owens or Jim Thorpe). But there are also biographies about individuals who have been trailblazers in some respect. For instance, Benjamin Banneker was one of America's first African American mathematicians; he also developed a very accurate farmer's almanac (see *Dear Benjamin Banneker* [Pinkney 1994]). *We the People: Navajo Code Talkers* (Santella 2004) documents the story of the Navajo military participants who developed a code during World War II based on the Navajo language; the code was important to the war effort because it was not broken by the Japanese. Documentation about the role of the code talkers was kept secret until 1969; only in 2001 were code talkers recognized by the President and awarded medals for their service.

We are certainly not suggesting that all biographies have potential for mathematics instruction. But mathematics teachers might work with language arts or social studies teachers to identify those biographies of individuals from different cultures for which mathematics tasks can be developed. (We list several possible biographies at the end of this chapter.)

Summary

Resources like the Olympic Games, Masks of the World, Flags of the World, and various biographies can capture the spirit of many cultural groups and their "totality," as Davis (2006) phrases it, giving culture a visible presence in the classroom when such resources are included in the curriculum as part of instruction. Including such resources can motivate and engage students, too many of whom dislike mathematics and fail to see how it relates to their own lives. The Equity Principle from the *Principles and Standards for School Mathematics* (NCTM 2000) recommends that teachers have high expectations and provide support for all students. Using cultural resources is one approach to engage all students in mathematics.

References

Cool Runnings. 1993. Written by Lynn Siefert and Michael Ritchie. Directed by Jon Turteltaub. Produced by Dawn Steel. Walt Disney Productions. Film.

Davis, Bonnie M. 2006. *How to Teach Students Who Don't Look Like You: Culturally Relevant Teaching Strategies*. Thousand Oaks, CA: Corwin Press.

Faul, Michael A. 1997. *The Story of Africa & Her Flags to Color*. Santa Barbara, CA: Bellerophon Books.

Jones, Joan Cohen. 2000. "Using Flags to Teach Mathematics Concepts and Skills." In *Changing the Faces of Mathematics: Perspectives on African Americans*, edited by Marilyn E. Strutchens, Martin L. Johnson, and William F. Tate, 151–56. Reston, VA: National Council of Teachers of Mathematics.

Ladson-Billings, Gloria. 1995. "Making Mathematics Meaningful in a Multicultural Context." In *New Directions for Equity in Mathematics Education*, edited by Walter G. Secada, Elizabeth Fennema, and Lisa B. Adajian, 126–45. New York: Cambridge University Press.

National Council of Teachers of Mathematics. 2000. *Principles and Standards for School Mathematics*. Reston, VA: NCTM.

Oxlade, Chris. 2005. *Eyewitness: Olympics*. New York: Dorling Kindersley.

Pinkney, Andrea Davis. 1994. *Dear Benjamin Banneker*. San Diego: Gulliver Books.

Santella, Andrew. 2004. *We the People: Navajo Code Talkers*. Minneapolis, MN: Compass Point Books.

The Jesse Owns Story. 1984. Written and Produced by Harold Gast. Directed by Richard Irving. Paramount Pictures. Film.

Wiest, Lynda R. 2001. "Teaching Mathematics from a Multicultural Perspective." *Equity and Excellence in Education* 34: 16–25.

Wilma. 1977. Directed and produced by Bud Greenspan. National Broadcasting Company.

Possible Biographies

Adler, David A. 2000. *A Picture Book of Sacagawea*. New York: Holiday House.

Bruchac, Joseph. 1994. *A Boy Called Slow: The True Story of Sitting Bull*. New York: Putnam & Grosset.

Crawford, Bill. 2005. *All American: The Rise and Fall of Jim Thorpe*. Hoboken, NJ: John Wiley & Sons.

Lasky, Kathryn. 1994. *The Librarian Who Measured the Earth*. Boston: Little, Brown and Company.

———. 2000. *Vision of Beauty: The Story of Sarah Breedlove Walker*. Cambridge, MA: Candlewick Press.

Lumpkin, Beatrice. 1991. *Senefer: A Young Genius in Old Egypt*. Trenton, NJ: Africa World Press, Inc.

Lyons, Mary E. 1993. *Stitching Stars: The Story Quilts of Harriet Powers*. New York: Charles Scribner's Sons.

McKissack, Patricia C. 1997. *A Picture of Freedom: The Diary of Clotee, a Slave Girl*. New York: Scholastic.

Ponte, Fred A. n.d. *Kamehameha the Great*. Lihue, HI: Island Printers.

Rumford, James. 2004. *Sequoyah: The Cherokee Man Who Gave His People Writing*. Boston: Houghton Mifflin.

Stanley, Diane. 1988. *Shaka: King of the Zulus*. New York: Morrow Junior Books.

Weatherford, Carole Boston. 2007. *Jesse Owens: Fastest Man Alive*. New York: Walker & Company.

Media References

Aardema, Verna. 1975. *Why Mosquitoes Buzz in People's Ears.* New York: Puffin Pied Paper Books.

Akeelah and the Bee. 2006. Produced by Nancy Hult Ganis, Sid Ganis, Laurence Fishburne, Michael Romerse, and Danny Llewelyn. Written and Directed by Doug Atchison. 112 minutes. Lionsgate. Film.

A Raisin in the Sun. 1961. Produced by David Susskind and Philip Rose. Directed by Daniel Petric. Written by Lorraine Hansberry. 128 minutes. Columbia Pictures. Videocassette.

A Raisin in the Sun. 2008. Produced by John M. Eckert. Directed by Kenny Leon. 131 minutes. Sony Pictures Television. Film.

Bruchac, Joseph. 1999. *Seeing the Circle.* Katonah, NY: Richard C. Owen.

Castañeda, Omar S. 1993. *Abuela's Weave.* New York: Lee & Low Books.

Children of Heaven. 1999. Produced by Institute for the Intellectual Development of Children and Young Adults. Written and Directed by Majid Majidi. 88 minutes. Miramax Films. Film.

Freedman, Russell. 2006. *The Adventures of Marco Polo.* New York: Authur A. Levine.

Goble, Paul. 1984. *Buffalo Woman.* New York: Aladdin.

Goodman, Robert, and Robert A. Spicer (Adapted by). 1974. *Issunbōshi.* Aiea, HI: Island Heritage.

Grifalconi, Ann. 1986. *The Village of Round and Square Houses.* Boston: Little, Brown and Company.

Harris, Zoe, and Suzanne Williams. 1998. *Piñatas & Smiling Skeletons: Celebrating Mexican Festivals.* Berkeley, CA: Pacific View Press.

Krull, Kathleen. 2004. *Harvesting Hope: The Story of Cesar Chavez.* San Diego: Harcourt.

Lancaster Museum of Art. 2002. *Masks from Around the World: The Collection of Robert A. Ibold.* Lancaster, PA: Lancaster Museum of Art.

Lasky, Kathryn. 2000. *Vision of Beauty: The Story of Sarah Breedlove Walker.* Cambridge: Candlewick.

Lumpkin, Beatrice. 1991. *Senefer: A Young Genius in Old Egypt.* Trenton, NJ: African World Press.

McBrier, Page. 2001. *Beatrice's Goat.* New York: Atheneum.

McDermott, Gerald. 1974. *Arrow to the Sun.* New York: Viking.

McKissack, Patricia C. 1992. *A Million Fish . . . More or Less.* New York: Alfred A. Knopf.

Mendez, Phil. 1989. *The Black Snowman.* New York: Scholastic.

No More Baths. 2003. Produced by Rick V. Larsen and Jeff T. Miller. Written and Directed by Timothy J. Nelson. 93 minutes. Feature Films for Families. Film.

Perez, L. King. 2002. *First Day in Grapes*. New York: Lee & Low Books.

Pilkington, Doris. 1996. *Follow the Rabbit-Proof Fence*. Brisbane, Australia: University of Queensland Press.

Rabbit-Proof Fence. 2002. Produced by Philip Noyce and Christine Olson. Directed by Philip Noyce. 94 minutes. Miramax Films. Film.

Selena. 1997. Produced by Moctesuma Esparza. Written and Directed by Gregory Nava. 128 minutes. Warner Brothers. Film.

Somaiah, Rosemarie (Retold by). 2006. "Munna and the Grain of Rice." In *Indian Children's Favourite Stories*, 8–15. Tokyo: Tuttle.

Sonneborn, Liz. 2003. *The Cherokee*. New York: Franklin Watts of Scholastic.

Spirit of the Animals. 1989. Produced by Jan C. Nickman. Written and Directed by Kathleen Phelan. 90 minutes. Miramar Images. Film.

The Lost Child. 2000. Produced by Richard Welsh. Directed by Karen Arthur and Teleplay by Sally Beth Robinson. 98 minutes. Hallmark Hall of Fame Productions. Film.

The Pursuit of Happyness. 2006. Produced by Todd Black, Jason Blumenthal, Steve Tisch, James Lassiter, and Will Smith. Directed by Gabriele Muccino. 117 minutes. Columbia Pictures. Film.

The Way Home. 2002. Produced by Jae-woo Hang and Woo-hyun Hang. Written and Directed by Jeong-Hyang Lee. 80 minutes. CJ Entertainment. Film.

Under the Same Moon. 2008. Produced by Patricia Riggen and Gerardo Barrera. Written by Ligiah Villalobos and Directed by Patricia Riggen. 110 minutes. Twentieth Century Fox. Film.

www.flags.net/fullindex.htm

www.masksoftheworld.com

www.topics-mag.com/edition11/games-section.htm

http://library.thinkquest.org/J0110166/index.html

www.gameskidsplay.net

www.soccerballworld.com

http://national.soccerhall.org/US_NationalTeamRec_Intro.htm

www.womensprosoccer.com

http://worldstadiums.com